LADIES' HOME JOURNAL

HANDBOOK
OF HOLIDAY
CUISINE

LADIES' HOME JOURNAL
HANDBOOK OF HOLIDAY CUISINE

MARGARET HAPPEL
ELSA HARRINGTON

DOWNE PUBLISHING, INCORPORATED
NEW YORK

CONTENTS

Introduction VII
Appetizers and Canapes 1
Soups 19
Holiday Meats 37
Vegetables 67
Welcome Winter Salads 87
Confections and Cookies 103
Breads and Cakes 123
Light Holiday Desserts 145
Festive Drinks 167
Menus 179
Table of Weights and Measures 186
Correct Measuring Techniques 187
Index of Recipes by Chapter 189
General Index 193

We would like to thank Ann Vehslage for her way
with words, Lynn St. John for his expert photography,
and Binnie L. Weissleder for her creative design.
MEH & EMH

INTRODUCTION

Consider the special qualities of the holidays that stretch from Thanksgiving to Twelfth Night: the festive gatherings, the celebrated traditions—all in some way depend on the most delicious, glorious food imaginable.

These are *the* holidays during the year when entertaining is at its most active and inspired . . . when treasured visions of sugarplums — or, indeed of complete feasts — become delectably real.

Surprisingly, no one, until now, has ever gathered together a complete compendium of recipes created just for these holidays. Hence, this *Ladies' Home Journal Handbook of Holiday Cuisine,* a collection of over 200 kitchen-tested recipes that constitute a first-ever selection of dishes brimming with mid-winter holiday cheer.

No matter in what fashion you celebrate these festive days of autumn and early winter— be it with a family gathering or with an all-out, once-a-year crowd scene — here are dishes to satisfy the most discerning palate.

This is a true cook's tour, with every recipe you'll ever need for the marvelous meals of the season: appetizers and canapes, some hot, others cold; exotic soups with an international flavor; holiday meats (our perfect turkey has a lovely maple glaze) and vegetables; winter salads; sweets, such as candies and cookies, ideal for giving (and *keeping*); traditional breads and cakes; desserts with the light touch; party drinks — they're all here, and all yours for the making.

Fully aware as we are that this time of year makes many demands on valuable time, we've made simplicity one of the watchwords throughout the book. Modern "convenience" products go into the recipes wherever they can create maximum good taste (with minimum fuss) *and* help keep the cook from spending long hours at the stove.

To help you further enjoy all the gaiety that's going on around you, a goodly half of the recipes may in some way be prepared in advance. So . . . no more last-minute frenzies in the kitchen when you'd like to be greeting and enjoying your guests.

In a few cases, the recipes call for rather esoteric ingredients. Truffles, for instance, are an ingredient in a pâté recipe, but the alternative of chopped ripe olives is suggested, should truffles be impractical. This kind of wily substitution takes place wherever and whenever necessary.

As you want to have the very best and most interesting meals possible, the last chapter is one of twelve traditional menus, each well-balanced as is, but flexible enough to suit individual needs and tastes. All make maximum use of the recipes in the book. We've touched each of our menus with imagination and each basic style of holiday entertaining is represented, from the easy informality of an open house, brunch or trim-the-tree party to the precise elegance of a formal, sit-down dinner.

Here is a Chanukah meal with all the proper touches, a true Greek holiday feast, a fine, old-fashioned Thanksgiving dinner. Christmas and New Year's, representing many things to as many people, receive understandable emphasis in our menu planning, and you'll be pleased, we feel, to combine your favorite ideas with ours. Perhaps you'll come across some new traditions to add to your own. And so, without further ado, permit us to serve up the gayest, most carefree, most delicious holiday season ever.

CHAPTER ONE / APPETIZERS AND CANAPES

Appetizers and canapes, whatever the occasion, should serve to whet, rather than dull, the appetite. When served at a large stand-up party the tasty morsels in this chapter may be offered in plentiful supply. Some are ideal "finger food," while others are more formal, and should be served as a first course at a sit-down dinner. Several may be served either way, such as the Caviar Eggs, the Escargots and the Angels in Blankets. Just place them on small, individual plates and garnish prettily with watercress or parsley.

ESCARGOTS

1 escargot kit containing 18 snail shells and 1 (7 ½ -oz.) tin snails
¼ cup softened butter or margarine
¼ cup finely chopped parsley
1 Tb. lemon juice
2 tsp. crushed garlic
1 tsp. finely chopped shallot
1 tsp. salt
¼ tsp. pepper
⅛ tsp. nutmeg

Rinse snail shells with hot water and set aside to dry. Drain snails thoroughly, then place 1 in each shell.

To make snail butter, combine ¼ cup each softened butter or margarine and finely chopped parsley, 1 tablespoon lemon juice, 2 teaspoons crushed garlic, 1 teaspoon finely chopped shallot, 1 teaspoon salt, ¼ teaspoon pepper and ⅛ teaspoon nutmeg. Divide mixture over snails in shells. Place snails in sectioned snail plates or in an oven-proof serving dish and bake about 10 minutes at 425°, or until butter sauce begins to bubble. Serve at once, with crusty French bread. *(See photograph.)*

❄ *Note:* Clams (you'll need 12) may be substituted for the snails in this recipe. Chop clams coarsely, place in snail shells (or on clam shells) and spread with snail butter prepared as in above recipe. Top with fresh bread crumbs and bake about 10 minutes as above.

ANGELS IN BLANKETS

36 shrimp, shelled and deveined
18 slices bacon, cut in half
⅓ cup prepared mustard

Wash and dry thoroughly 36 shelled and deveined shrimp. Spread each of 18 bacon slices, cut in half, with about ½ teaspoon prepared mustard. Wrap shrimp in a prepared, halved bacon slice and secure with a toothpick. Preheat broiler for 5 minutes; broil shrimp 6 inches from heat 3 to 4 minutes. Turn and broil 2 or 3 minutes longer. Serve hot. *(See photograph.)*

SAUTÉED CAULIFLOWERETTES

2 ½ cups cauliflowerettes (1 medium head)
1 cup butter or margarine
1 garlic clove, crushed
1 ½ tsp. bottled garlic salt with parsley
1 ½ tsp. lemon pepper

Break 1 medium head cauliflower into bite-sized flowerettes, to make 2½ cups. Wash and dry thoroughly. In a large skillet, melt 1 cup butter or margarine and add 1 garlic clove, crushed. Add cauliflowerettes and sauté gently 10 or 15 minutes, or until tender but still crisp. Drain on paper towels.
Combine 1½ teaspoons each bottled garlic salt with parsley, and lemon pepper, and sprinkle over cauliflower. Serve warm. (These may be kept warm for no longer than 30 minutes, in a 300° oven.) (See photograph.)

❈ Note: No fresh cauliflower? Use 2 (10-oz.) pkgs. frozen cauliflower, thawed and dried thoroughly with paper towels.

VAN DYKE RADISHES WITH GREEN BUTTER

36 radishes
¾ cup softened, unsalted butter or margarine
2 Tb. finely chopped parsley
1 Tb. finely chopped watercress
1 tsp. grated onion

Remove stems and "tails" of 36 radishes. Wash and dry well. Using a sharp paring knife, cut each radish in half crosswise in an up and down, zig-zag pattern.
Combine ¾ cup softened, unsalted butter or margarine with 2 tablespoons finely chopped parsley, 1 tablespoon finely chopped watercress and 1 teaspoon grated onion.
Fill center of each radish half with some of the green butter, or place green butter in a pastry tube or bag with a star tip and pipe a small rosette onto each radish half. Makes 72. (See photograph.)

3

CAVIAR EGGS

12 hard-cooked eggs
1 cup sour cream
1 tsp. grated lemon rind
½ cup red caviar
Watercress

Peel and chill 12 hard-cooked eggs. Combine 1 cup sour cream and 1 teaspoon grated lemon rind and mix well. To serve, cut eggs in half lengthwise and spoon 2 teaspoons sour cream mixture into each. Top with 1 teaspoon red caviar per egg half. Garnish with watercress. Makes 24 halves. *(See photograph.)*

COCONUT CHEESE BITES

1 (8-oz.) pkg. cream cheese, softened
1 (4-oz.) pkg. blue cheese, crumbled
1 cup coconut, toasted

In a medium-sized bowl, mix 1 (8-oz.) pkg. softened cream cheese with 1 (4-oz.) pkg. blue cheese, crumbled. Form into bite-sized morsels, using about 2 teaspoons each.
Spread 1 cup coconut on a baking sheet and "toast" 10 to 12 minutes at 325°, until golden. Remove from baking sheet, cool and crumble slightly. Toss cheese bites in coconut to coat lightly. Chill before serving. Makes about 2 dozen.

GARLIC-SALTED NIBBLES

4 cups honeycomb cereal
½ cup butter or margarine
2 tsp. bottled garlic salt with parsley

Spread 4 cups honeycomb cereal on a baking sheet. Melt ½ cup butter or margarine and pour over cereal. Bake 5 or 6 minutes at 325°, or until crisp, stirring once.
Remove from oven and pour into a bowl. Sprinkle cereal with 2 teaspoons bottled garlic salt with parsley and toss lightly to mix. Serve warm.

4

CRABMEAT QUICHE

2 (7 ½ -oz.) cans crabmeat (2 cups)
2 cups coarsely grated Swiss cheese (½ lb.)
1 (10-oz.) pkg. pie crust mix
6 eggs
3 cups light cream
½ cup dry sherry
1 Tb. salt
1 tsp. nutmeg
½ tsp. pepper

Pick over crabmeat from 2 (7½-oz.) cans, discarding any bits of shell. Flake crabmeat and toss lightly with 2 cups coarsely grated Swiss cheese. Set aside.

Prepare 1 (10-oz.) pkg. pie crust mix and roll out on a lightly floured surface to an 18 x 12-inch rectangle. Fit into a 15½ x 10½ x 1-inch jelly roll pan. Spoon combined crabmeat and cheese into crust. Combine 6 eggs, 3 cups light cream, ½ cup dry sherry, 1 tablespoon salt, 1 teaspoon nutmeg and ½ teaspoon pepper. Beat well. Pour over crabmeat in pie crust and bake 15 minutes at 425°. Reduce heat to 325° and bake 20 to 30 minutes more or until knife inserted in center of custard comes out clean. Serve warm, cut in 1 x 2-inch rectangles. Makes 150 pieces.

❋ Note: This may be prepared in advance in two steps. First, the crabmeat and cheese may be spooned into the pie crust, then well-covered and refrigerated. Second, the custard mixture may be prepared and covered and refrigerated. Remove both from refrigerator about 30 minutes before baking. Beat custard mixture well before pouring over crabmeat and bake as instructed above. If any quiche is left over (and we doubt there will be!), it may be reheated, covered with foil, 10 to 15 minutes at 325°.

You may use 2 cups cooked, fresh crabmeat, or 2 cups frozen crabmeat, defrosted, instead of the canned.

BABY BURGERS ON MINI-BISCUITS

BABY BURGERS:
½ lb. ground round steak
½ cup chopped onion
½ cup fresh bread crumbs
¼ cup milk
1 egg
2 Tb. chopped parsley
1 tsp. salt
½ tsp. Worcestershire sauce
⅛ tsp. pepper
3 Tb. creamy blue cheese
2 Tb. butter or margarine

MINI-BISCUITS:
2 cups buttermilk biscuit mix
½ cup cold water

To make baby burgers: Combine ½ lb. ground round steak with ½ cup chopped onion, ½ cup fresh bread crumbs, ¼ cup milk, 1 egg, 2 tablespoons chopped parsley, 1 teaspoon salt, ½ teaspoon Worcestershire sauce and ⅛ teaspoon pepper. Mix well. Shape into 36 (1-inch) balls, nesting ¼ teaspoon of the creamy blue cheese in the center of each, and enclosing completely; then flatten into 36 patties. In a large skillet, brown patties well on each side in 2 tablespoons butter or margarine.

To make mini-biscuits: Prepare 2 cups buttermilk biscuit mix according to label directions, using ½ cup cold water. Roll out ½ inch thick and cut with a 1½-inch biscuit cutter. Bake as directed. Makes 36 mini-biscuits. Split biscuits open and place burger in middle. Serve hot with any desired relish or mustard.

GUACAMOLE WITH WINTER VEGETABLES

2 medium-sized ripe avocados
1 cup diced, peeled tomato
¼ cup finely chopped scallions
2 Tb. finely chopped canned chili peppers or 2 tsp. chili powder
2 Tb. lemon juice
1 tsp. cumin
1 tsp. salt
⅛ tsp. pepper

Peel and mash 2 medium-sized ripe avocados. Add 1 cup diced, peeled tomato, ¼ cup finely chopped scallions, 2 tablespoons finely chopped canned chili peppers (or 2 teaspoons chili powder), 2 tablespoons lemon juice, 1 teaspoon cumin, 1 teaspoon salt and ⅛ teaspoon pepper. Mix well. Press plastic wrap closely over surface of guacamole to prevent it from darkening. Chill until serving. Makes 3 cups.

Serve with carrot sticks, cauliflowerettes, cucumber sticks, cherry tomatoes and radishes.

✻ *Note:* This also serves admirably as a spread on toast fingers, circles or triangles. For garnish, use parsley sprigs or sliced cherry tomatoes, shredded carrots or olive slices.

SMOKED SALMON AND AVOCADO

1 large, ripe avocado
12 thin slices smoked salmon
6 lime wedges
Black pepper

Peel and cut in half 1 large, ripe avocado. Cut each half into 6 wedges, placing 2 wedges on an individual serving plate. Arrange a slice of smoked salmon over each wedge and garnish with a lime wedge. Pass the pepper grinder so that each person may have a grind of fresh pepper. Serves 6.

CAVIAR CROUSTADE

8 slices firm white bread, toasted
1 (8-oz.) pkg. cream cheese, softened
2 Tb. lemon juice
⅛ tsp. hot pepper sauce
4 hard-cooked eggs
¼ cup chopped parsley
2 (4-oz.) jars red caviar
½ cup chopped green onion

Cut a 2 x 3-inch rectangle from each of 8 toast slices and set aside. Combine 1 (8-oz.) pkg. cream cheese, softened, with 2 tablespoons lemon juice and ⅛ teaspoon hot pepper sauce. Set aside. Separate egg white from egg yolks of 4 hard-cooked eggs; chop the whites fine and push the yolks through sieve. Spread each toast slice with cream cheese mixture. Make a ⅛-inch border of chopped parsley around the edge of each toast slice. Across the top of each arrange a band of sieved egg yolk, chopped green onion, red caviar and chopped egg white. Garnish with lemon or lime wedges. Serves 8. *(See photograph.)*

❋ *Note:* Black caviar may be substituted for the red called for here. You'll need 3 (2-oz.) jars.

BLUE CHEESE CANAPES

½ lb. blue cheese, crumbled (1 cup)
⅓ cup finely chopped mushrooms
¼ cup butter or margarine
2 garlic cloves, crushed
¼ tsp. black pepper

Beat together until smooth ½ lb. blue cheese, crumbled, ⅓ cup finely chopped mushrooms, ¼ cup butter or margarine, 2 garlic cloves, crushed, and ¼ teaspoon black pepper. Chill before using as a topping to spread over small melba toast rounds or individual rounds of pumpernickel bread. Makes 4 dozen.

SEVICHE OF SCALLOPS

Seviche is a very popular South American appetizer in which raw fish is marinated and "cooked" in citrus juices. Delicious!

2 lbs. filet of sole
½ lb. bay scallops
½ cup lemon juice
½ cup lime juice
1 cup quartered thin red onion slices
1 cup thin green pepper strips
1 tsp. salt
¼ tsp. pepper
¼ tsp. hot pepper sauce

Cut 2 lbs. filet of sole into 1-inch squares. Place in a large glass or china bowl and add ½ lb. bay scallops, ½ cup each lemon juice and lime juice. Toss well. Add 1 cup each quartered thin red onion slices and thin green pepper strips, 1 teaspoon salt and ¼ teaspoon each pepper and hot pepper sauce.

Toss to mix well. Cover and refrigerate at least 8 hours, or overnight. Stir gently three or four times. To serve, spoon into individual glass dishes or scallop shells. Sprinkle with parsley. Serves 6. (See *photograph.*)

BACON-MUSHROOM BOUCHÉES

¼ cup diced raw bacon
1 ½ cups coarsely chopped mushrooms
1 Tb. chopped parsley
1 Tb. lemon juice
2 tsp. all-purpose flour
⅛ tsp. black pepper

Sauté ¼ cup diced raw bacon until crisp. Remove with slotted spoon. Drain bacon on paper towel. In remaining fat sauté 1 ½ cups coarsely chopped mushrooms 2-3 minutes. Stir in 1 tablespoon each chopped parsley and lemon juice, 2 teaspoons all-purpose flour and ⅛ teaspoon black pepper. Add bacon. Mound on 48 (1 ½-inch) toast rounds or use to fill 48 tiny puff pastry shells. Keep hot until serving time. Makes 4 dozen.

HAM ROULADEN IN PIQUANT MAPLE SAUCE

9 thin slices boiled ham (about 1 lb.)
2 Tb. prepared mustard
1 cup cooked quick-cooking rice
¼ cup chopped hazelnuts
2 Tb. chopped parsley
1 tsp. grated lemon rind
1 tsp. celery salt
⅛ tsp. coarsely ground pepper

1 cup maple blended syrup
2 Tb. lemon juice
1 tsp. Worcestershire sauce
4 drops hot pepper sauce
6 lemon wedges

Spread each of 9 thin slices boiled ham with a little prepared mustard using 2 tablespoons in all. Combine 1 cup cooked quick-cooking rice with ¼ cup chopped hazelnuts, 2 tablespoons chopped parsley, 1 teaspoon each grated lemon rind and celery salt and ⅛ teaspoon coarsely ground pepper. Roll up each slice jellyroll fashion and secure with toothpicks.

In a skillet, mix 1 cup maple blended syrup with 2 tablespoons lemon juice, 1 teaspoon Worcestershire sauce and 4 drops hot pepper sauce. Bring to a boil; reduce heat and simmer 5 minutes. Add rolled, stuffed ham slices (rouladen), cover, and simmer 10 minutes.

Remove rouladen from sauce and cut each in half. Remove toothpicks and arrange 3 hot rouladen on individual serving plates. Spoon a little of the sauce over and serve with a lemon wedge. Serves 6.

HAWAIIAN CURRIED PORK

2 Tb. butter or margarine
¼ cup finely chopped celery
2 Tb. finely chopped onion
2 Tb. finely chopped green pepper
1 whole garlic clove
½-1 tsp. curry powder
1 cup chicken broth
½ cup maple blended syrup
2 Tb. cornstarch
1 (16-oz.) can crushed pineapple, well drained (juice reserved)
2 cups diced, cooked pork
1 (10-oz.) pkg. frozen puff pastry shells

Sauté until tender, in 2 tablesoons butter or margarine, ¼ cup finely chopped celery, 2 tablespoons each finely chopped onion and finely chopped green pepper, 1 whole garlic clove and ½ to 1 teaspoon curry powder. Remove and discard garlic.

To vegetables add 1 cup chicken broth and ½ cup maple blended syrup. Blend 2 tablespoons cornstarch with juice reserved from 1 (16-oz.) can crushed pineapple, well drained. Add to hot mixture and cook, stirring constantly, until sauce is thickened and clear. Add 2 cups diced, cooked pork and crushed pineapple, well drained. Simmer 10 minutes or until meat is heated through.

Meanwhile, prepare 1 (10-oz.) pkg. frozen puff pastry shells according to directions. Spoon pork mixture into hot puff pastry shells and serve at once. Serves 6.

TURKEY SALAD WITH SAUTÉED WALNUTS

4 cups diced, cooked turkey
1 cup chopped celery
1 cup mayonnaise
2 Tb. light cream
2 Tb. tarragon vinegar
1 tsp. salt
⅛ tsp. pepper
1 cup chopped walnuts
2 Tb. butter or margarine
Lettuce leaves

Combine 4 cups diced, cooked turkey and 1 cup chopped celery. Blend 1 cup mayonnaise with 2 tablespoons each light cream and tarragon vinegar, 1 teaspoon salt and ⅛ teaspoon pepper. Add to turkey, toss lightly to mix well and chill.

Sauté 1 cup chopped walnuts in 2 tablespoons butter or margarine until crisp and golden. Drain thoroughly on paper towels. Just before serving, stir ¾ cup of the nuts into the salad. Arrange salad on lettuce leaves and sprinkle with remaining ¼ cup nuts. Serves 6.

❉ Note: Chopped pecans or hazelnuts may be substituted for the walnuts, and, of course, chicken (or a mixture of chicken and turkey) may replace the turkey . . . a fine way to use up leftover holiday poultry. Cooked poultry, by the way, may be diced and frozen for future use.

If preferred the Turkey Salad can be dressed with a less rich and creamy dressing made by blending ⅔ cup olive or salad oil, ¼ cup tarragon vinegar, 1 garlic clove, crushed, 1 teaspoon salt and ¼ teaspoon each black pepper, dry mustard, paprika and grated lemon rind.

OLIVES AND MUSHROOMS AEGEAN

2 cups sliced raw mushrooms
1 ½ cups canned sliced ripe olives (a 5 ¾ -oz. can)
1 cup sliced celery
¼ cup lemon juice
1 garlic clove, crushed
1 tsp. oregano, crumbled
1 tsp. salt
½ tsp. cinnamon
¼ tsp. coarsely ground pepper
⅛ tsp. powdered cloves
1 cup olive oil
Lettuce

Gently toss to combine well 2 cups sliced raw mushrooms, 1 ½ cups canned, sliced ripe olives, drained, and 1 cup sliced celery. In a separate container or jar, mix ¼ cup lemon juice, 1 garlic clove, crushed, 1 teaspoon each oregano, crumbled with fingers, and salt, ½ teaspoon cinnamon, ¼ teaspoon coarsely ground pepper and ⅛ teaspoon powdered cloves. Mix well; add 1 cup olive oil and stir or shake vigorously. Pour over vegetables, tossing to coat well. Let stand at room temperature at least 1 hour. Chill before serving on lettuce. Serves 6. *(See photograph.)*

HORS D'OEUVRE PROVENCAL

2 large tomatoes, cut in eighths
1 (9-oz.) pkg. frozen artichoke hearts, cooked and drained
1 (7-oz.) can tuna, drained and flaked
1 cup Italian-style salad dressing
Watercress or lettuce

In a large bowl, gently toss to combine 2 large tomatoes, cut in eighths, 1 (9-oz.) pkg. frozen artichoke hearts, cooked and drained, and 1 (7-oz.) can tuna, drained and flaked. Pour 1 cup Italian-style salad dressing over mixture. Cover and chill at least 1 hour. Divide between 6 individual platters lined with watercress or lettuce. Serves 6.

13

CHICKEN LIVER BOATS

1 lb. chicken livers
2 Tb. butter or margarine
1 cup sliced mushrooms
1 tsp. grated onion
½ cup flour
2 ½ cups chicken broth
½ cup dry sherry
¼ cup lemon juice

6 small club rolls
2 Tb. butter or margarine
½ garlic clove, crushed

Cut 1 lb. chicken livers in half. Sauté in 2 tablespoons butter or margarine 5 minutes; add 1 cup sliced mushrooms and 1 teaspoon grated onion and sauté 5 minutes longer. Combine ½ cup flour with ½ cup of the chicken broth, mixing until smooth. Add remaining 2 cups chicken broth, mixing well, and add to chicken livers and cook, stirring constantly, until mixture is thickened. Just before serving, add ½ cup dry sherry and ¼ cup lemon juice.

To make "boats": Remove tops from 6 small club rolls. Scoop out center dough to leave a wall about ½ inch thick. Heat 2 tablespoons butter or margarine with ½ garlic clove, crushed, until butter melts. Brush garlic butter over inside of rolls and bake 8 to 10 minutes at 375°, to heat and crisp the rolls. To serve, spoon the piping-hot chicken liver mixture into the hot "boats." Serves 6.

❈ *Note:* You may substitute 1 lb. calves' liver, cut into ¼ x ½-inch strips, for the chicken livers.

BOURBON PÂTÉ

1 ½ lbs. liverwurst
1 cup butter or margarine
¼ cup bourbon
½ tsp. pepper
1 (2-oz.) can black truffles, chopped, or ½ cup chopped,
   pitted black olives

Let 1 ½ lbs. liverwurst and 1 cup butter or margarine stand at room temperature until soft enough to mash—about 1 hour for the liverwurst.

Mash liverwurst with a fork until free of lumps. Add butter or margarine and mix well. Add ¼ cup bourbon, ½ teaspoon pepper and 1 (2-oz.) can black truffles, chopped (or ½ cup chopped, pitted black olives), and mix thoroughly. Pack into a crock or lightly oiled 1-qt. mold. Chill.

Serve directly from crock or mold, or unmold onto serving plate. Serve with crackers, toast rounds or quartered slices of hot, lightly buttered toast. Serves 6.

✳ *Note:* Truffles are expensive, and a similar effect can be achieved by using chopped black olives.

SALMON PÂTÉ

1 (16-oz.) can pink salmon
1 cup finely diced carrot
⅔ cup sliced green onion
¼ cup butter or margarine, softened

Drain 1 (16-oz.) can pink salmon, reserving liquid. Place a small amount of salmon in blender and whir with a small amount of 1 cup finely diced carrot, ⅔ cup sliced green onion, ¼ cup softened butter or margarine and some of the reserved salmon liquid. Whir until smooth. Place in bowl. Repeat this step until all salmon, carrot, green onion, butter or margarine and salmon liquid are used up. Press into a 1-qt. mold or crock. Unmold or keep in crock, as desired, when serving. Serve with crisp breads and crackers. Serves 6 to 8 generously.

15

VEGETABLE HORS D'OEUVRE WITH
CHICKEN LIVER STUFFING

¼ lb. chicken livers
2 Tb. butter or margarine
¼ cup chopped onion
¼ cup chopped celery
¼ cup chopped carrots
¼ cup chopped mushrooms
2 Tb. light cream
2 Tb. brandy
½ tsp. dried tarragon
¼ tsp. dried chervil
¼ tsp. salt
1 cup pkgd. herb-seasoned dry bread stuffing

Wash ¼ lb. chicken livers. Pat dry with paper towels. Over medium heat sauté livers in 2 tablespoons butter or margarine 5 minutes or until barely pink when cut. Remove to blender.
Sauté ¼ cup chopped onion 5 minutes; add to livers. Add ¼ cup each chopped celery, carrots and mushrooms, 2 tablespoons each light cream and brandy, ½ teaspoon dried tarragon leaves, ¼ teaspoon dried chervil and ¼ teaspoon salt.
Blend mixture at high speed for 3 minutes or until mixture is smooth. Add 1 cup pkgd. herb-seasoned dry bread stuffing. Blend 10 seconds.
For hors d'oeuvre, using small spoon or pastry bag, fill small whole mushroom caps or cherry tomato halves with liver mixture. Bake at 350° for 10 minutes. Makes 40 to 50 hors d'oeuvre.

BEEF LINDSTROM

6 slices rye bread
¼ cup butter or margarine
1 lb. ground round steak
½ cup finely chopped canned beets from 1 (8-oz.) can
½ cup finely chopped onion
2 Tb. beet juice
2 Tb. heavy cream
1 Tb. drained, chopped capers
1 egg yolk
1 tsp. salt
¼ tsp. pepper

Toast 6 slices rye bread and spread each with some of the ¼ cup butter or margarine. Combine 1 lb. ground round steak with ½ cup each finely chopped beets, and finely chopped onion, 2 tablespoons each beet juice and heavy cream, 1 tablespoon drained, chopped capers, 1 egg yolk, 1 teaspoon salt and ¼ teaspoon pepper. Mix well.

Spread beef mixture over toast slices and broil 6 inches from heat 5 to 8 minutes, depending on rareness desired. Makes 6 openface sandwiches.

❊ *Note:* Any bread you like may be used here—rye bread is the traditional type served in Sweden.

CHAPTER TWO / SOUPS

A bowl of soup, served with a salad and a light fruit dessert, can be a marvelous meal in itself, a pause in holiday activity. That same bowl of soup, be it piping hot or chilled, can also be the beginning of a lavish holiday feast. Either way, here are some of the best soups around, many inspired by recipes from faraway places (Belgium, China, Hungary, to name a few). As you try these recipes, you'll find that our judicious use of modern "convenience" products will enable you to come up with soups that really taste of hours of slow cooking on the back burner.

BURGUNDY BEEF SOUP

In this and in any of our soup recipes calling for beef broth, consommé or bouillon, 1 cup broth may be made up from dehydrated powder or a cube (or measured from a can) and water.

2 (10½-oz.) cans condensed consommé
2 (10½-oz.) cans water
1 cup thinly sliced mushrooms
½ cup julienne-cut carrots
½ cup thinly sliced celery
½ cup fresh or frozen peas
½ cup dry domestic Burgundy
2 Tb. lemon juice
½ cup chopped parsley

In a large saucepan, combine 2 (10½-oz.) cans each condensed consommé and water, 1 cup thinly sliced mushrooms and ½ cup each julienne-cut carrots, thinly sliced celery and fresh (or frozen) peas. Bring to a boil, reduce heat, cover and simmer 10 minutes. Remove from heat and stir in ½ cup dry domestic Burgundy and 2 tablespoons lemon juice. Sprinkle with ½ cup chopped parsley and serve. Serves 12 to 16. *(See photograph.)*

EGGNOG SOUP

4 cups commercial eggnog
¼ cup dry sherry
2 tsp. grated orange rind
1 tsp. grated lemon rind
1 egg white
1 tsp. sugar
¼ tsp. salt
Nutmeg

In a medium bowl, combine 4 cups commercial eggnog, ¼ cup dry sherry, 2 teaspoons grated orange rind and 1 teaspoon grated lemon rind. Mix well and chill. In a small bowl, beat 1 egg white until it forms soft peaks. Add 1 teaspoon sugar and ¼ teaspoon salt and beat until a stiff, glossy meringue is formed.
To serve, top each bowl of soup with a dollop of meringue and dust lightly with nutmeg. Serves 6.

COCK-A-LEEKIE SOUP

1 (4-lb.) chicken
8 cups water
2 cups coarsely chopped onion
2 cups (1-inch) celery chunks with leaves
½ cup chopped parsley
10 peppercorns
2 whole cloves
1 bay leaf
1 Tb. salt
½ tsp. thyme
¼ cup barley
8 leeks

In a large kettle, place 1 (4-lb.) chicken, 8 cups water, 2 cups each coarsely chopped onion and 1-inch celery chunks with leaves, ½ cup chopped parsley, 10 peppercorns, 2 whole cloves, 1 bay leaf, 1 tablespoon salt and ½ teaspoon thyme. Bring to a boil, reduce heat, cover and simmer 2 hours, or until chicken is tender. Remove chicken and set aside to cool. Strain broth and return to kettle.

Add ¼ cup barley to broth and bring to a boil. Reduce heat, cover and simmer 30 minutes. Meanwhile, remove and discard tough outer leaves of 8 leeks. Cut off green tops to within 1 inch of white stems and discard. Slice white stems into ½-inch pieces and add to broth after broth has simmered 30 minutes. Simmer, covered, 15 minutes more and set aside.

Remove skin from cooled chicken. Remove meat and cut into bite-sized pieces. Return chicken pieces to soup and cook gently until chicken is heated through. Serves 6 to 8.

BOOKBINDER'S SHRIMP CHOWDER

½ cup finely chopped onion
½ cup butter or margarine
¼ cup flour
2 tsp. salt
½ tsp. white pepper
¼ tsp. mace
4 cups light cream
½ lb. small shrimp, shelled and deveined
1 (7-oz.) pkg. crabmeat, thawed and drained
¼ cup dry sherry

In upper part of double boiler, over direct heat, sauté ½ cup finely chopped onion in ½ cup butter or margarine until onions are soft but not brown. Remove from heat, add ¼ cup flour, 2 teaspoons salt, ½ teaspoon white pepper and ¼ teaspoon mace. Stir until smooth and well blended. Stir in 4 cups light cream and cook over direct heat stirring until thickened.

Add ½ lb. small shrimp, shelled and deveined, and place over hot (not boiling) water. Cook, uncovered, 15 to 20 minutes, or until shrimp are cooked. Add 1 (7-oz.) pkg. crabmeat, thawed and drained, 5 minutes before end of cooking time. Just before serving stir in ¼ cup dry sherry. Serves 6. *(See photograph.)*

JELLIED MADRILÈNE

2 (12½-oz.) cans madrilène
½ cup Madeira
½ cup heavy cream
½ tsp. salt

Warm 2 (12½-oz.) cans madrilène just until soup liquefies. Remove from heat, stir in ½ cup Madeira and chill at least 4 hours, or overnight.

Break up jellied madrilène with a fork and serve in soup bowls (or sherbet or parfait glasses). Just before serving, beat ½ cup heavy cream and ½ teaspoon salt until cream is stiff. Top each serving of soup with some of the salted whipped cream. Serves 6.

BLACK BEAN SOUP WITH RUM AND MAPLE

½ cup finely chopped onion
2 Tb. butter or margarine
2 (10 ½ -oz.) cans black bean soup
2 (10 ½ -oz.) cans water
¼ cup maple blended syrup
¼ cup dark rum
2 hard-cooked eggs, chopped
6 lemon slices

In a medium saucepan, sauté ½ cup finely chopped onion in 2 tablespoons butter or margarine until onion is golden. Stir in 2 (10½-oz.) cans each black bean soup and water, mixing well. Heat until piping hot but do not boil. Remove from heat and stir in ¼ cup each maple blended syrup and dark rum. Garnish each serving with a spoonful of chopped egg (from 2 hard-cooked eggs, chopped) and a lemon slice. Serves 6.

✳ *Note:* If you prefer, 2 tablespoons lemon juice may be substituted for the dark rum.

QUICK BORSCHT WITH POTATO

6 small potatoes, unpeeled
1 cup chopped onion
1 garlic clove, crushed
2 Tb. butter or margarine
1 (16-oz.) can diced beets, drained
½ cup beet juice
1 (10 ½ -oz.) can beef bouillon
1 Tb. cider vinegar

Boil 6 small potatoes, unpeeled, ½ hour, or until tender; drain and set aside. Sauté 1 cup chopped onion and 1 garlic clove, crushed, in 2 tablespoons butter or margarine until onion is golden. Drain 1 (16-oz.) can diced beets, reserving ½ cup juice, and add to onion and garlic along with 1 (10½-oz.) can beef bouillon (or consommé) and 1 tablespoon cider vinegar. Heat until piping hot, but do not boil.
Peel the hot potatoes and place 1 potato in each soup bowl, ladling soup over. Serve at once. Serves 6.

SAUSAGE AND ONION SOUP

½ lb. sausage meat
1 cup chopped onion
½ cup chopped celery
½ cup (1-inch) strips green pepper
¼ cup cornmeal
2 cups water
1 Tb. salt
½ tsp. pepper
1 cup heavy cream
2 Tb. lemon juice or lime juice
2 Tb. butter or margarine
2 Tb. chopped parsley

Crumble ½ lb. sausage meat into a medium saucepan and cook, stirring, until meat is lightly browned. Pour off all but 2 tablespoons fat. Add 1 cup chopped onion and ½ cup each chopped celery and 1-inch strips green pepper. Cook, stirring, until onion is transparent.

Combine ¼ cup cornmeal with 1 cup of the water and add to sausage mixture. Add remaining 1 cup water, 1 tablespoon salt and ½ teaspoon pepper, bring to a boil, reduce heat and simmer 5 minutes, stirring constantly. Cook 10 minutes more, stirring once or twice. Stir in 1 cup heavy cream and simmer 5 minutes. Just before serving, stir in 2 tablespoons lemon juice (or lime juice). Combine 2 tablespoons each butter or margarine and chopped parsley and mix well. Top each serving of hot soup with some of this parsley butter. Serves 6.

✤ *Note:* To use ½ lb. sausage links in this recipe, remove meat from the casings and crumble as directed above. Brown-and-serve sausages could also be used, but change the method as follows: brown sausage, then slice. Set aside and add to soup 5 minutes before serving. Meanwhile, sauté onion, celery and green pepper in 2 tablespoons butter or margarine, and proceed as directed.

CHINESE SOUP

4 (10 ½-oz.) cans chicken broth
¼ cup cider vinegar
2 Tb. sugar
3 tsp. soy sauce
3 eggs
¼ cup finely shredded spinach leaves
¼ cup paper-thin celery slices
12 to 18 paper-thin radish slices

Chill 4 (10½-oz.) cans chicken broth at least ½ hour. Open and remove all congealed chicken fat. Place in a saucepan and stir in ¼ cup cider vinegar, 2 tablespoons sugar and 2 teaspoons of the soy sauce.

Beat 3 eggs with remaining 1 teaspoon soy sauce. Pour into a lightly oiled loaf pan (7 ½ x 3¾ x 2¼-inches) and cover tightly with foil. Set on a rack in a larger pan containing 1 inch boiling water. Simmer 20 minutes, or until custard is firm and a knife inserted in center comes out clean. Remove from heat, discard foil and let custard cool. With a sharp knife, cut cooled custard into 6 squares.

To serve, heat soup but do not boil. In each of 6 soup bowls place 1 square of custard, 2 teaspoons finely shredded spinach leaves (from ¼ cup), 2 teaspoons paper-thin celery slices (from ¼ cup) and 2 or 3 paper-thin radish slices. Pour hot soup into bowls and serve at once. Serves 6.

❊ Note: If you can find a Japanese soup powder called "dashi-no-moto", which comes in bags much like our tea bags, use 1 large bag and 4 cups boiling water in place of the 4 cans chicken broth and the 2 teaspoons soy sauce. The powder is available in Oriental food stores.

BELGIAN BEER SOUP

1 cup coarsely chopped carrots
1 cup sliced celery
1 cup chopped onion
¼ cup butter or margarine
2 (11 ¼ -oz.) cans split pea soup with ham
1 (12-oz.) can or bottle beer
1 cup beef broth

In a large saucepan, sauté 1 cup each coarsely chopped carrots, sliced celery and chopped onion in ¼ cup butter or margarine 10 minutes. Add 2 (11¼-oz.) cans split pea soup with ham, 1 (12-oz.) can (or bottle) beer and 1 cup beef broth. Mix well and simmer 10 minutes, or until beer stops foaming. Serve hot. Serves 6.

DOUBLE MUSHROOM CONSOMMÉ

3 (10 ½ -oz.) cans beef broth
2 cups chopped mushrooms
1 cup cold water
1 tsp. salt
¼ cup dry sherry
1 cup thinly sliced mushrooms
2 Tb. butter or margarine

Slowly heat 3 (10½-oz.) cans beef broth in a medium saucepan. In a small saucepan combine 2 cups chopped mushrooms with 1 cup cold water and 1 teaspoon salt. Bring to a boil, reduce heat, cover and simmer 5 minutes. Remove from heat and let stand 5 minutes.
Strain, pressing mushrooms firmly with back of a spoon to extract as much juice as possible. Add strained mushroom juice and ¼ cup dry sherry to broth. Sauté 1 cup thinly sliced mushrooms in 2 tablespoons butter or margarine 3 minutes; drain. Just before serving, place some of the sautéed mushroom slices in each soup bowl, then pour hot sherried broth into each. Serves 6 to 8.

WATERCRESS SOUP

4 envelopes or cubes chicken bouillon
4 cups boiling water
½ cup chopped watercress
Lemon or lime wedges

Dissolve 4 envelopes (or cubes) chicken bouillon in 4 cups boiling water in a medium saucepan. Add ½ cup chopped watercress and bring to a boil, stirring constantly. Cover, remove from heat and let stand 5 mintues. Stir and serve at once with a lemon or lime wedge. Serves 6.

HUNGARIAN CHERRY SOUP

1 (30-oz.) can pitted dark sweet cherries
1 cup domestic pink Chablis
¼ cup lemon juice
¼ cup maple blended syrup
½ cup sour cream
1 Tb. grated lemon rind

Put contents of 1 (30-oz.) can pitted dark sweet cherries, with juice, in blender container and whir. Pour into a bowl and stir in 1 cup domestic pink Chablis and ¼ cup each lemon juice and maple blended syrup. Mix well and chill. Top each serving with a dollop of sour cream (from ½ cup) and a sprinkle of grated lemon rind (from 1 tablespoon). Serves 6.

✻ *Note:* A headier version of this soup is made by heating the cherries with 1 (1-inch) stick cinnamon, 4 cloves and 1 large twist lemon peel. Remove spices from cherries before pureeing. Heat and thicken with 1 tablespoon cornstarch; stir in 2 cups Burgundy wine before adding remaining ingredients. Chill.

NAVAJO CORN SOUP

1 (17-oz.) can cream style corn
2 cups light cream
1 cup finely chopped celery with leaves
½ tsp. pepper
¼ tsp. mace
6 drops hot pepper sauce

Combine thoroughly 1 (17-oz.) can cream style corn with 2 cups light cream, 1 cup finely chopped celery with leaves, ½ teaspoon pepper, ¼ teaspoon mace and 6 drops hot pepper sauce. Chill. Serves 6.

WHITE RUSSIAN CHOLODNIK

4 cups buttermilk
1 cup diced, cooked shrimp
¾ cup diced, seeded, unpeeled cucumber
1 garlic clove, crushed
1 tsp. grated onion
1 tsp. dried dill or 2 tsp. chopped fresh dill
1 tsp. salt
½ tsp. powdered fennel
¼ tsp. white pepper

Combine 4 cups buttermilk, 1 cup diced, cooked shrimp, ¾ cup diced, seeded, unpeeled cucumber, 1 garlic clove, crushed, 1 teaspoon grated onion, 1 teaspoon dried dill (or 2 teaspoons chopped fresh dill), 1 teaspoon salt, ½ teaspoon powdered fennel, and ¼ teaspoon white pepper. Let stand at room temperature at least 30 minutes to allow flavors to blend. Chill before serving. Serves 6 to 8.

BAYOU BISQUE

1 cup chopped onion
1 whole garlic clove, peeled
2 Tb. butter or margarine
2 cups chicken broth
1 tsp. salt
½ tsp. nutmeg
½ tsp. allspice
½ tsp. coriander
¼ tsp. pepper
2 cups light cream
1 ½ cups canned pumpkin
1 cup canned chopped tomatoes, well drained (8-oz. can)

In a medium saucepan, sauté 1 cup chopped onion and 1 whole garlic clove, peeled, in 2 tablespoons butter or margarine. Remove garlic and discard. Stir in 2 cups chicken broth, 1 teaspoon salt, ½ teaspoon each nutmeg, allspice and coriander, and ¼ teaspoon pepper. Bring to a boil, reduce heat, cover and simmer 15 minutes.

Meanwhile, combine 2 cups light cream with 1 ½ cups canned pumpkin, mixing well until smooth. When chicken broth mixture has simmered 15 minutes, stir in cream and pumpkin mixture and add 1 cup canned chopped tomatoes, well drained. Heat gently until very hot (do not boil) and serve. Serves 6.

❋ *Note:* This soup is also delicious served cold. How to? After chicken broth mixture has simmered 15 minutes, remove from heat and stir in cream and pumpkin mixture and the canned chopped tomatoes. Cool, then chill thoroughly, and stir well just before serving.

PURÉE MONGOLE

2 ½ cups light cream
1 (10 ¾ -oz.) can tomato soup
1 (11 ¼ -oz.) can pea soup
½ tsp. curry powder
1 slice white bread
1 Tb. butter or margarine

Combine 2½ cups light cream, 1 (10¾-oz.) can tomato soup,
1 (11¼-oz.) can pea soup, and ½ teaspoon curry powder.
Heat until piping hot, but do not boil.
Meanwhile, cut crust from 1 slice white bread and cut bread into
small dice. Sauté in 1 tablespoon butter or margarine until crisp
and golden. Serve hot soup with croutons sprinkled over the top.
Serves 6.

SHRIMP AND OYSTER CHOWDER

1 (10-oz.) can frozen cream of shrimp soup
1 (10-oz.) can frozen oyster stew
1 (10 ¼ -oz.) can frozen potato soup
2 cups light cream
1 cup milk
½ tsp. thyme
¼ tsp. white pepper
2 Tb. butter or margarine
Paprika

In a large saucepan, heat 1 (10-oz.) can each frozen cream of
shrimp soup and frozen oyster stew and 1 (10¼-oz.) can frozen
potato soup until all soups are thawed, stirring frequently. Stir
in 2 cups light cream, 1 cup milk, ½ teaspoon thyme and ¼ teaspoon white pepper. Heat but do not boil. Top each serving of
hot chowder with 1 teaspoon butter or margarine (from 2 tablespoons) and a dash of paprika. Serves 6 to 8.

Bookbinder's
Shrimp Chowder

Escargots
Sautéed Cauliflowerettes
Angels in Blankets

Caviar
Croustades

Olives and
Mushrooms
Aegean

Seviche of
Scallops

Caviar Eggs
Van Dyke Radishes
with Green Butter

Burgundy
Beef Soup

BEEF AND ALE SOUP

1 (1-oz.) pkg. beef gravy mix
2 (10 ½ -oz.) cans beef bouillon
2 cups water
¼ cup ale or beer

In a medium saucepan, combine 1 (1-oz.) pkg. beef gravy mix, 2 (10½-oz.) cans beef bouillon and 2 cups water. Bring to a boil, stirring constantly. Remove from heat and stir in ¼ cup ale (or beer). Serve at once. Serves 6.

RINDSUPPE (Brown Beef Soup)

2 cups chopped onion
1 garlic clove, crushed
2 Tb. butter or margarine
¾ lb. ground lean beef
¼ lb. beef liver, cut into ½ -inch cubes
½ cup diced carrots
½ cup diced celery
½ cup diced potatoes
¼ cup chopped parsley
1 bay leaf
1 Tb. salt
½ tsp. pepper
6 envelopes beef broth mix
6 cups cold water

Sauté 2 cups chopped onion and 1 garlic clove, crushed, in 2 tablespoons butter or margarine. Add ¾ lb. ground lean beef, ¼ lb. beef liver, cut into ½-inch cubes, ½ cup each diced carrots, diced celery and diced potatoes, ¼ cup chopped parsley, 1 bay leaf, 1 tablespoon salt, ½ teaspoon pepper, 6 envelopes beef broth mix and 6 cups cold water.
Bring mixture to a boil, stirring once or twice. Reduce heat, cover and simmer 15 minutes, or until vegetables are just tender. Serves 10 to 12.

CHAPTER THREE / HOLIDAY MEATS

At the heart of any great meal is a memorable meat course. It is on this that you undoubtedly spend the most time and money, and the rich variety of the recipes that follow is worthy of both. Each is full of the proper gala spirit of the season, be it formal or informal. The chapter begins, fittingly, with that best-loved bird, the turkey (which Brillat-Savarin, the great French gastronome, considered the finest of all gifts from the New World to the Old). Beyond that we have some elegant and innovative ideas that are sure to answer the endless quest for something really different—even spectacular—for a culinary *pièce de résistance*. If you have any questions about the proper times and temperatures for roasting meat or fowl, consult our chart on page 186, which has all the answers.

MAPLE-GLAZED TURKEY WITH
PECAN CORNBREAD STUFFING

1 (12- to 15-lb.) turkey
1 (16-oz.) pkg. cornbread stuffing
2 Tb. butter or margarine
1 cup coarsely chopped pecans or walnuts
¼ tsp. ginger
1 cup soft butter or margarine
2 cups water
1 cup thinly sliced onion

Turkey neck and giblets (gizzard, heart, liver)
4 cups water
1 celery stalk, chopped
1 onion, cut in pieces
1 tsp. salt
½ tsp. pepper
1 ¾ cups maple blended syrup
Water or chicken broth
¾ cup flour
Salt and pepper

Rinse with cold water and drain thoroughly 1 (12- to 15-lb.) turkey. Prepare 1 (16-oz.) pkg. cornbread stuffing according to directions. In 2 tablespoons butter or margarine, sauté 1 cup coarsely chopped pecans (or walnuts) 5 minutes, stirring constantly. Stir in ¼ teaspoon ginger. Add to prepared cornbread stuffing and toss lightly to mix well.

Fill neck cavity of bird with 1 ½ to 2 cups stuffing. Bring neck skin over stuffing and fasten to back of bird with a metal or wooden skewer. Fill body cavity with remaining stuffing and close by sewing with a large needle and heavy thread, or by securing with 3 or 4 skewers and lacing them closed with string. Tie ends of leg together.

Place turkey, breast up, in roasting pan and rub all over with 1 cup soft butter or margarine. Pour 2 cups water into pan and add 1 cup thinly sliced onion. Roast 3 to 3½ hours at 325°, basting frequently with pan juices.

Meanwhile, place turkey neck and giblets (except liver) in a saucepan with 4 cups water, 1 celery stalk, chopped, 1 onion, cut in pieces, 1 teaspoon salt and ½ teaspoon pepper. Bring to a boil, then reduce heat and simmer 1½ hours. Add turkey liver and simmer ½ hour more. Remove gizzard, heart and liver and chop coarsely. Remove meat from neck and discard bones. Strain broth and set aside.

Remove turkey from roasting pan and set in a shallow pan lined with heavy-duty foil. Pour 1¾ cups maple blended syrup over turkey and return to oven in foil-lined pan. Roast 1 hour more, basting every 15 minutes with syrup. Serves 10 to 12.

Gravy: Skim as much fat at possible from pan drippings in roasting pan and set aside. Add de-fatted drippings to strained giblet broth. Measure and add enough water or chicken broth to make up 6 cups liquid.

Return 4 tablespoons fat to roasting pan and, while off heat, stir in ¾ cup flour, blending until mixture is smooth. Add 6 cups liquid and cook, stirring constantly, until mixture comes to a boil and is thickened. Strain into a saucepan and stir in chopped giblets and neck meat and salt and pepper to taste. Simmer 10 minutes. Makes about 6 cups gravy. *(See photograph.)*

Garnish: Break young green leaves from 2 bunches celery into sprigs. Place in ice water and refrigerate to crisp. Cut peel from 6 to 8 oranges in one continuous strip. Roll each into a spiral to form a "rose". Secure peel in position with toothpick. Let turkey stand at room temperature for 15 minutes before carving. Arrange garnish at last moment. *(See photograph.)*

ROAST CAPON WITH APPLE AND RAISIN STUFFING

¼ cup butter or margarine
1 cup chopped celery
½ cup chopped onion
4 cups pared, chopped tart apple (4 apples)
2 cups herb-seasoned croutons
1 cup golden raisins
2 garlic cloves, crushed
1 tsp. salt
½ tsp. pepper
1 (6 lb.) capon
½ cup soft butter or margarine
1 cup dry vermouth
1 cup water
1 cup chopped onion

GRAVY:
Chicken broth
6 Tb. flour
Salt and pepper

In ¼ cup butter or margarine, sauté 1 cup chopped celery and ½ cup chopped onion until onion is transparent. In a large bowl, combine celery and onion with pan juices, 4 cups pared, chopped apple, 2 cups herb-seasoned croutons, 1 cup golden raisins, 2 garlic cloves, crushed, 1 teaspoon salt and ½ teaspoon pepper.

Fill neck cavity of 1 (6-lb.) capon with about ¾ cup stuffing. Bring neck skin over stuffing and fasten to back of bird with a metal or wooden skewer. Fill body cavity with remaining stuffing and close cavity by sewing with a large needle and heavy white thread. Tie ends of legs together.

Place capon, breast side up, in roasting pan. Rub all over with ½ cup soft butter or margarine. Pour 1 cup dry vermouth and 1 cup water into roasting pan and add 1 cup chopped onion. Roast 3 hours at 325°, basting often.

Remove capon from oven and place on warm platter. Keep warm while you prepare gravy. Serves 6.

Gravy: Skim all fat from pan juices and set aside. Measure pan juices and add enough chicken broth to make 3 cups. Return 2 tablespoons fat to roasting pan. While off heat add 6 tablespoons flour, stirring until smooth. Stir in 3 cups liquid. Cook, stirring, over medium heat until mixture comes to a boil and is thickened. Strain and add salt and pepper. Makes 3 cups gravy.

DUCK MONTMORENCY

1 (17-oz.) can Bing cherries
1 cup tawny port
2 (4-lb.) ducks, quartered
4 large cubes sugar
1 large orange
2 Tb. cornstarch

Drain 1 (17-oz.) can Bing cherries and place cherries in a medium bowl. Add 1 cup tawny port, cover and let stand at room temperature 3 to 4 hours (preferably overnight).

Wash and dry 2 (4-lb.) ducks, quartered. Prick skin well with a sharp fork. Broil duck, skin side up, 6 inches from source of heat until all surface fat has run off—20 to 25 minutes. Remove from broiler and arrange in large baking pan. Roast in oven another 30 minutes at 350°.

Meanwhile, rub 4 large sugar cubes firmly over 1 orange to remove zest and aromatic oils from skin. Squeeze orange and measure ¼ cup juice. Add juice to 2 tablespoons cornstarch and stir until smooth. In a saucepan, combine cherries and port with cornstarch mixture. Cook, stirring constantly, until liquid is thick and clear. Add sugar cubes and stir to dissolve.

Arrange duckling quarters on a warm platter. Spoon sauce over duckling and serve some alongside. Serves 6.

ROAST GOOSE WITH SAGE AND ONION STUFFING

1 (8- to 10-lb.) goose
1 cup dry white wine
1 cup water
½ cup chopped onion
1 garlic clove, sliced

GRAVY:
2 Tb. goose fat
Chicken broth
6 Tb. flour
Salt and pepper

Wash and dry 1 (8- to 10-lb.) goose. Fill neck cavity with 1 cup Sage and Onion Stuffing (recipe follows) and secure neck skin to back of bird with a metal or wooden skewer. Fill body cavity with remaining stuffing and close opening.

Prick entire surface of goose with a sharp-tined fork. Place goose, breast side up, in roasting pan. Pour 1 cup each dry white wine and water into pan and add ½ cup chopped onion and 1 garlic clove, sliced. Roast 30 minutes to the pound at 325°, basting every 30 minutes. (If goose becomes browned to your liking before cooking time is completed, cover loosely with foil.) Remove goose from oven and allow to "rest" for 15 minutes before carving.

Gravy: Skim fat from pan drippings, reserving 2 tablespoons. Pour off pan drippings and add enough chicken broth to make up 3 cups liquid. Return reserved 2 tablespoons goose fat to roasting pan and, while off heat, add 6 tablespoons flour, blending until smooth. Stir in 3 cups liquid and cook, stirring, over medium heat until mixture comes to a boil and is thickened. Strain and add salt and pepper to taste. Makes 3 cups.

SAGE AND ONION STUFFING

2 cups chopped onion
¼ cup butter or margarine
2 cups coarsely chopped mushrooms
¼ cup chopped parsley
2 tsp. powdered sage
½ tsp. pepper
1 (16-oz.) pkg. herb stuffing mix, water, butter or margarine

Sauté 2 cups chopped onion in ¼ cup butter or margarine until onions are transparent. Add 2 cups coarsely chopped mushrooms, ¼ cup chopped parsley, 2 teaspoons powdered sage and ½ teaspoon pepper. Sauté, stirring, 2 or 3 minutes more. Prepare 1 (16-oz.) pkg. herb stuffing using water and butter or margarine according to directions. Add onion and mushroom mixture and toss lightly to mix thoroughly. Makes 6 cups stuffing.

ROAST RACK OF LAMB

1 (14-chop) saddle of lamb
2 cups fresh bread crumbs
4 garlic cloves, crushed
1 cup chopped parsley
½ cup olive oil
2 tsp. salt
1 tsp. powdered rosemary
½ tsp. pepper

Ask your butcher to cut 1 (14-chop) saddle of lamb into 2 racks, to "French" the bones and to crack the ribs at the backbone. Trim off all fat.
Combine 2 cups fresh bread crumbs, 4 garlic cloves, crushed, 1 cup chopped parsley, ½ cup olive oil, 2 teaspoons salt, 1 teaspoon powdered rosemary, and ½ teaspoon pepper. Mix well. Firmly press half of this mixture across surface of each rack. Place meat in shallow roasting pan and roast 30 minutes at 400° for very rare lamb. For well-done lamb, increase cooking time to 45 minutes. Serves 6. (See photograph.)

BLANQUETTE OF POULTRY

¼ cup butter or margarine
1 cup diced carrots
1 cup chopped onion
2 (10 ½-oz.) cans cream of chicken soup
1 cup light cream
1 tsp. salt
½ tsp. thyme
¼ tsp. white pepper
3 cups cubed, cooked chicken
3 cups cubed, cooked turkey
2 egg yolks
2 Tb. lemon juice
6 buttered, heart-shaped toast slices

In ¼ cup butter or margarine, sauté 1 cup each diced carrots and chopped onion 8 to 10 minutes, until onion is transparent. Stir in 2 (10½-oz.) cans cream of chicken soup, 1 cup light cream, 1 teaspoon salt, ½ teaspoon thyme and ¼ teaspoon white pepper. Mix well.

Add 3 cups each cubed, cooked chicken and turkey and heat gently until meat is heated through . . . about 8-10 minutes. Remove from heat. Beat thoroughly 2 egg yolks. Slowly beat ¼ cup hot sauce mixture into yolks. Return this mixture to blanquette, add 2 tablespoons lemon juice and mix well. Serve at once with buttered heart-shaped toast slices. Serves 6.

❋ *Note:* For elaborate festive presentation the classic garnish is a formal arrangement of tiny heart-shaped croutons of fried bread or puff pastry, small lemon wedges and crisp bacon rolls. It is a garnish designed to give crispness and texture to a very smooth and creamy dish.

STANDING RIB ROAST WITH YORKSHIRE PUDDING

1 tsp. dry mustard
1 (4-lb.) 2-rib "Newport" roast of beef

GRAVY:
¼ cup flour
2 cups beef bouillon

A "Newport" roast is one which is purchased with the rib ends (short ribs) removed.
Rub half of 1 teaspoon dry mustard into each side of 1 (4-lb.) 2-rib "Newport" roast of beef. Place meat in a roasting pan and roast 1¾ hours at 325°. Turn off oven and allow meat to stand in oven 15 minutes. Remove and keep warm. Serves 6.
Gravy: Gently pour off all but about 2 tablespoons pan drippings. While off heat, stir in ¼ cup flour, mixing until smooth. Add 2 cups beef bouillon and cook, stirring, until mixture comes to a boil and is thickened. Strain. Makes about 2 cups gravy.

❋ Note: A favored accompaniment to beef, along with Yorkshire Pudding (recipe follows), are oven-roast potatoes. Parboil 6 to 8 pared white potatoes about 10 minutes. Drain well and arrange in roasting pan around beef 45 minutes before end of cooking time. Turn several times.

YORKSHIRE PUDDING

2 Tb. cooking oil
2 eggs
1 cup milk
1 cup sifted flour
1 tsp. salt
⅛ tsp. pepper

Pour 2 tablespoons cooking oil into a 9x9x2-inch pan. In a medium bowl, beat with a rotary beater 2 eggs, 1 cup each milk and sifted flour, 1 teaspoon salt and ⅛ teaspoon pepper.
Set oiled pan in oven preheated to 425° and leave in oven 3 to 5 minutes. Remove and immediately pour batter into pan. Bake 25 to 30 minutes, or until pudding is rich golden brown. Cut into squares and serve immediately with roast beef. Serves 6.

HAM EN CROÛTE

1 (12- to 15-lb.) ham on the bone, fully cooked
¼ cup prepared spicy mustard
4 (10-oz.) pkgs. pie crust mix
2 tsp. powdered thyme
2 tsp. powdered sage
½ tsp. pepper
1 cup ice water
2 egg yolks
2 Tb. heavy cream

Skin 1 (12- to 15-lb.) ham on the bone, fully cooked, and remove all fat. Spread ham with ¼ cup prepared spicy mustard. In a large bowl, mix 4 (10-oz.) pkgs. pie crust mix with 2 teaspoons each powdered thyme and sage and ½ teaspoon pepper. Add 1 cup ice water mixing lightly. Shape into a ball. On a large, well-floured surface, roll out dough to ¼-inch thickness. Place ham in center of dough and wrap dough around it. Trim off any excess dough. Moisten edges of pastry with water, join and seal securely. Roll out trimmed pieces of dough and cut into decorative shapes with cookie cutter. Moisten backs of shapes with water and place on pastry-wrapped ham.

In a small bowl, beat with a fork 2 egg yolks and 2 tablespoons heavy cream. Brush over pastry. Bake ham 45 minutes at 375°, or until crust is golden brown. Serves 24.

❀ Note: If the ham is served hot, Madeira Sauce is an excellent accompaniment. Heat together ½ cup each red wine and beef consommé, 2 tablespoons each chopped parsley, chopped onion and chopped celery, ⅛ teaspoon each pepper and thyme. Simmer 5 minutes. Strain and whisk into a mixture of 1 tablespoon each butter or margarine and flour which have been heated in a saucepan for 3 to 4 minutes until golden brown in color. Boil until reduced by half and add ½ cup Madeira wine.

HAM WITH GELATINE GLAZE

1 (3-lb.) canned ham, chilled thoroughly
1 (13 ¾ -oz.) can chicken broth
1 (3-oz.) pkg. lemon-flavored gelatine
2 Tb. lemon juice
2 Tb. dry sherry
Dill sprigs
Thin carrot slices
Thin white turnips, sliced
Pitted black olives, sliced

Remove from can and place on a wire rack set on a large baking sheet 1 (3-lb.) ham, chilled thoroughly.

Bring to a boil 1 (13¾-oz.) can chicken broth. Pour over 1 (3-oz.) pkg. lemon-flavored gelatine and stir to dissolve. Cool. Stir in 2 tablespoons each lemon juice and dry sherry and chill until the mixture is consistency of unbeaten egg white. Using a large spoon, coat ham evenly with gelatine mixture. Chill until glaze is firm. Melt remaining gelatine mixture over hot water and chill once again to the consistency of egg white.

Remove glazed ham from refrigerator and gently press sprigs of dill onto surface. Brush with remaining chilled gelatine mixture. Dip flower shapes cut from thin carrot and turnip slices into gelatine and arrange on ham. Dip pitted black olive slices into gelatine mixture and arrange on "flowers". Chill 1 hour before serving. Serves 8 to 12.

❋ *Note:* If you wish, a 12- to 15-lb. fully-cooked ham on the bone, with surface fat removed, may be used for either of our festive glazes (see Brandied Cream Cheese Glaze, page 49), in which case the glaze recipes should be doubled.

STEAK AND KIDNEY PIE WITH OYSTERS

2 cups chopped onion
2 garlic cloves, crushed
¼ cup butter or margarine
1 (2-lb.) piece stewing beef
1 tsp. instant meat tenderizer
1 cup water
1 bay leaf
1 whole clove
10 peppercorns
1 lb. beef kidneys
1 cup water
1 tsp. salt
1 (10½-oz.) can beef gravy
½ lb. fresh mushrooms, quartered, or 2 (4-oz.) cans sliced mushrooms
12 fresh oysters, shucked, or 1 (4-oz.) can oysters
1 (10-oz.) pkg. frozen puff pastry shells, thawed
1 egg yolk
1 Tb. milk

In a large saucepan, sauté 2 cups chopped onion and 2 garlic cloves, crushed, in ¼ cup butter or margarine until onion is transparent.

Next, moisten with water both sides of 1 (2-lb.) piece stewing beef and sprinkle each side with half of 1 teaspoon instant meat tenderizer. Pierce meat all over with a sharp-tined fork and cut into 1-inch cubes. Add to saucepan containing onion and garlic, with 1 cup water, 1 bay leaf, 1 whole clove and 10 pepper-corns. Bring to boil, reduce heat. Simmer, covered, 15 minutes. Meanwhile cut 1 lb. beef kidneys in half and remove all tubes and gristle. Cut into 1-inch dice and place in a small saucepan along with 1 cup water and 1 teaspoon salt. Bring to a boil and cook, uncovered, 5 minutes. Drain well and add to simmering beef mixture. Simmer 45 minutes more.

Stir in 1 (10½-oz.) can beef gravy, ½ lb. fresh mushrooms, quartered (or 2 [4-oz.] cans, sliced mushrooms drained), 12 fresh oysters, shucked (or 1 [4-oz.] can oysters) and ½ cup oyster liquor. Simmer 10 minutes, then pour into a large, shallow cas-serole and set aside.

Gently press together 6 individual shells from 1 (10-oz.) pkg. frozen puff pastry shells, thawed. Roll out to make a sheet of pastry 1 inch larger than top of casserole dish containing meat mixture. Trim off a ½-inch strip of dough all around. Moisten edge of casserole with water and press the ½-inch strip of dough onto edge of dish. Moisten this dough with water.

Fit top crust on over beef and kidney mixture and seal edges together. Cut fancy shapes from any dough trimmings. Moisten back of shapes with water and place on crust. Cut 2 or 3 slits in top of pastry to allow steam to escape and brush all over with a mixture of 1 egg yolk beaten with 1 tablespoon milk. Bake 20 minutes at 450°, or until crust is rich golden brown. Serves 6. (See photograph.)

HAM WITH BRANDIED CREAM CHEESE GLAZE

1 (5-lb.) canned ham, chilled thoroughly
2 (8-oz.) pkgs. cream cheese
1 (3-oz.) pkg. Roquefort cheese
¼ cup chopped parsley
¼ cup chopped chives
2 Tb. brandy

Remove from can and place on serving dish 1 (5-lb.) ham, chilled thoroughly. Keep chilled while making cream cheese glaze.

Let 2 (8-oz.) pkgs. cream cheese and 1 (3-oz.) pkg. Roquefort cheese stand at room temperature until soft—about 1 hour. In a medium bowl, combine softened cheeses, ¼ cup each chopped parsley and chopped chives and 2 tablespoons brandy. Mix until smooth (makes about 2¼ cups). Frost the ham with this mixture and chill again at least 1 hour to set cheese "frosting". Serves 16 to 20.

STUFFED VEAL SHOULDER

1 (10-oz.) pkg. frozen chopped spinach
½ cup water
1 cup chopped onion
1 garlic clove, crushed
¼ cup olive oil
1 ½ cups cooked rice
¼ cup pignoli nuts
1 tsp. salt
½ tsp. nutmeg
¼ tsp. pepper
1 (3 ½ - to 4-lb.) shoulder of veal, boned
1 cup water
1 cup dry vermouth
4 strips bacon
1 Tb. cornstarch

Cook 1 (10-oz.) pkg. frozen chopped spinach according to directions, using ½ cup water. Drain. Sauté 1 cup chopped onion and 1 garlic clove, crushed, in ¼ cup olive oil until onion is golden. Remove from heat and add 1 ½ cups cooked rice, ¼ cup pignoli nuts, 1 teaspoon salt, ½ teaspoon nutmeg and ¼ teaspoon pepper. Toss lightly with spinach to mix well.

Stuff 1 (3½- to 4-lb.) shoulder of veal, boned, with the spinach-rice mixture and place in a roasting pan with 1 cup each water and dry vermouth. Cover veal with 4 strips bacon. Roast 3½ hours at 325°, basting frequently. Serves 6.

To make gravy: Measure pan juices after skimming off all fat. Add water if necessary to make up 2 cups liquid. Stir in 1 tablespoon cornstarch blended in 2 tablespoons cold water. Cook, stirring constantly, until thickened. Makes about 2 cups.

❋ Note: If pignoli nuts are hard to find, substitute ¼ cup slivered almonds. Also, breast of veal may be used, instead of boned shoulder of veal. Ask your butcher to cut a pocket in the breast of veal and place spinach stuffing in pocket. To carve, meat should be sliced between the ribs and transferred from platter to plates with a pie server.

Ratatouille

Roast Rack
of Lamb

Maple Glazed
Turkey with
Pecan Cornbread
Stuffing

Steak and
Kidney Pie
with Oysters

Belgian Endive
with
Zingara Sauce

VITELLO TONNATO

If this recipe calls for what seems an inordinate amount of parsley for the tuna sauce, don't worry. It's supposed to!

1 (4-lb.) boned veal roast, rolled
1 (10½-oz.) can chicken broth
1 cup water
½ cup chopped onion
¼ cup chopped parsley
1 Tb. salt
1 tsp. pepper

TUNA SAUCE:
2 cups chopped parsley
1 cup chopped onion
6 garlic cloves
1 (7-oz.) can oil-packed tuna, undrained
½ cup olive oil
¼ cup butter or margarine, melted
¼ cup dry white wine
2 Tb. lemon juice
1 tsp. salt
1 tsp. grated lemon rind
½ tsp. pepper

In a large, heavy saucepan, place 1 (4-lb.) boned veal roast, rolled, 1 (10½-oz.) can chicken broth, 1 cup water, ½ cup chopped onion, ¼ cup chopped parsley, 1 tablespoon salt and 1 teaspoon pepper. Bring to a boil, reduce heat, cover and simmer gently 2 hours, or until meat is tender.

Tuna Sauce: Combine in blender 2 cups chopped parsley, 1 cup chopped onion, 6 garlic cloves, 1 (7-oz.) can oil-packed tuna, undrained, ½ cup olive oil, ¼ cup each butter or margarine melted and dry white wine, 2 tablespoons lemon juice, 1 teaspoon each salt and grated lemon rind and ½ teaspoon pepper. Whir at high speed 1 minute, or until smooth. Chill.

To serve, slice veal and arrange on warm platter. Spoon a band of chilled sauce down the center of meat and serve remaining sauce alongside. Serves 6 to 8.

VEAL PICCATA WITH SAFFRON RICE

1 (29-oz.) can Italian tomatoes with basil
½ cup flour
2 eggs
2 Tb. dry white wine
2 Tb. water
2 Tb. grated Parmesan cheese
1 Tb. chopped parsley
1 tsp. salt
¼ tsp. pepper
12 thin slices veal (2 to 2 ½ lbs.)
½ cup olive oil
¼ cup butter or margarine
¼ cup finely chopped onion
1 garlic clove, crushed

Break into pieces 1 (29-oz.) can Italian tomatoes with basil. Drain in sieve. Set aside. In a flat bowl, place ½ cup flour, 2 eggs, 2 tablespoons each dry white wine, water and grated Parmesan cheese, 1 tablespoon chopped parsley, 1 teaspoon salt and ¼ teaspoon pepper. Beat well with fork until smooth. Dip 12 slices thin veal, 1 at a time, into mixture, then sauté in a large skillet in a mixture of ½ cup olive oil and ¼ cup butter or margarine, until veal is golden brown on both sides. Remove and keep warm.

Add ¼ cup finely chopped onion and 1 garlic clove, crushed, to butter and oil remaining in skillet and cook until golden. Add reserved, strained tomatoes and cook, stirring, 5 minutes, until tomatoes are hot. Arrange cooked veal on a bed of Saffron Rice or Almond Wild Rice (recipes follow) and spoon hot tomatoes over meat. Serves 6.

SAFFRON RICE

½ cup chopped onion
1 garlic clove, crushed
¼ cup butter or margarine or olive oil
1 ½ cups long grain rice
3 ½ cups chicken broth
1 tsp. salt
⅛ tsp. powdered saffron

In a large skillet, sauté ½ cup chopped onion and 1 garlic clove, crushed, in ¼ cup butter or margarine (or olive oil) until onion is pale gold. Add 1 ½ cups long grain rice and mix well. Add 3½ cups chicken broth, 1 teaspoon salt and ⅛ tsp. powdered saffron. Bring to a boil, cover and reduce heat. Simmer 15 minutes, until all liquid is absorbed and rice is tender. Serves 6.

✳ *Note:* Saffron is very expensive, and may be omitted from this recipe . . . but there will be loss of flavor. The same coloring can be achieved, however, by adding 2 or 3 drops yellow food coloring when broth is added.

ALMOND WILD RICE

½ cup butter or margarine
1 cup coarsely chopped fresh mushrooms
1 cup raw brown and wild rice mix
½ cup slivered almonds
2 (10-oz.) cans beef consommé

In a large skillet, melt ½ cup butter or margarine and sauté 1 cup coarsely chopped mushrooms until tender. . . about 5 minutes. Add 1 cup brown and wild rice mix and ½ cup slivered almonds. Cook over medium heat until rice and almonds are toasted. Add 2 (10-oz.) cans beef consommé and bring to a simmer. Cook, covered, over low heat until all consommé is absorbed and rice is tender. Stir once or twice during cooking time. Serves 6.

CASSOULET

2 cups dried white beans
2 qts. water
6 slices bacon
2 cups chopped onion
2 garlic cloves, crushed
3 bay leaves
1 Tb. salt
1 tsp. thyme
1 tsp. pepper

¼ cup olive oil or cooking oil
2 cups chopped onion
4 garlic cloves, crushed
3 lbs. lamb, cut in 1 ½ -inch cubes
2 cups dry white wine
1 (10 ½ -oz.) can beef bouillon
1 (6-oz.) can tomato paste
1 (6-oz.) can water
¾ cup chopped parsley
2 tsp. thyme
1 tsp. rosemary

In a large saucepan combine 2 cups dried white beans and 2 qts. water. Boil 5 minutes; remove from heat and let stand 1 hour. Add 6 slices bacon cut in 1 ½ -inch pieces, 2 cups chopped onion, 2 garlic cloves, crushed, 3 bay leaves, 1 tablespoon salt and 1 teaspoon each thyme and pepper. Bring to a boil, reduce heat and simmer 1 ½ hours, stirring once or twice, until beans are tender. Drain and discard liquid.

Meanwhile, in a large, heavy pot or Dutch oven, heat ¼ cup olive oil (or cooking oil) and sauté 2 cups chopped onion and 4 garlic cloves, crushed, until onion is transparent. Push onion and garlic to one side of pot and add 3 lbs. lamb, cut in 1 ½ -inch cubes, and brown on all sides. Add 2 cups dry white wine, 1 (10½-oz.) can beef bouillon, 1 (6-oz.) can each tomato paste and water, ½ cup chopped parsley, 2 teaspoons thyme and 1 teaspoon rosemary. Bring to a boil, reduce heat, cover and simmer 1 hour.

Drain, reserving broth. In the bottom of a large, heat-proof casserole or Dutch oven, place ⅓ of the drained beans. Top beans with half the drained meat. Repeat layers, ending with beans on top. Pour reserved lamb broth over all. Bring once again to a boil, reduce heat, cover and simmer 1 hour more. To serve, sprinkle with remaining ¼ cup chopped parsley. Serves 6 to 8.

STUFFED PORK CHOPS WITH MAPLE-ORANGE SAUCE

6 rib pork chops, 1 inch thick
1 cup chopped celery
½ cup chopped onion
¼ cup butter or margarine
1 cup sliced mushrooms
1 tsp. salt
½ tsp. poultry seasoning
¼ tsp. pepper
1 cup maple blended syrup
½ cup orange juice

Ask your butcher to cut a pocket in each of 6 rib pork chops, 1 inch thick, and trim away all but about ⅛ inch fat.

Sauté 1 cup chopped celery and ½ cup chopped onion 5 minutes in 2 tablespoons of the ¼ cup butter or margarine. Add 1 cup sliced mushrooms and sauté 5 minutes more. Remove from heat and stir in 1 teaspoon salt, ½ teaspoon poultry seasoning and ¼ teaspoon pepper. Cool slightly, then spoon mixture into pockets in each pork chop.

In a heavy skillet sauté chops over low heat in remaining 2 tablespoons butter or margarine 5 minutes per side. Add 1 cup maple blended syrup and ½ cup orange juice to skillet, cover and simmer 20 minutes. Remove cover and continue cooking 10 minutes more, basting frequently with pan juices. Serves 6.

MEXICAN FLANK STEAK

1 (2- to 3-lb.) flank steak
1 Tb. instant meat tenderizer
2 tsp. chili powder
1 tsp. dry mustard
1 tsp. sugar
½ tsp. ground cumin
1 (12-oz.) can or bottle beer
1 cup chopped onion
1 garlic clove, crushed
2 Tb. olive oil or cooking oil
1 cup sliced mushrooms
½ cup diced, peeled tomatoes
2 cups packaged herb stuffing mix
1 tsp. salt
¼ tsp. pepper
1 cup water

Moisten with water 1 (2- to 3-lb.) flank steak on both sides and sprinkle each side with 1 ½ teaspoons instant meat tenderizer. Prick meat all over with a sharp-tined fork. Set aside. Combine 2 teaspoons chili powder, 1 teaspoon each dry mustard and sugar and ½ teaspoon ground cumin with 2 tablespoons of 1 (12-oz.) can beer. Spread on one side of tenderized steak.
Sauté 1 cup chopped onion and 1 garlic clove, crushed, in 2 tablespoons olive oil (or cooking oil) until onion is golden. Add 1 cup sliced mushrooms and ½ cup diced, peeled tomatoes and sauté 5 minutes more Add 2 cups packaged herb stuffing mix, 1 teaspoon salt and ¼ teaspoon pepper and toss lightly to mix well. Spread stuffing over steak and roll steak up, jelly roll fashion, starting with the smaller end. With strong, white cord or butcher's string tie rolled meat securely in 4 or 5 places.
Place on rack in baking pan. Pour remaining beer and 1 cup water into pan and roast 2 hours at 300°, basting meat frequently with pan juices. Place meat on a warm platter and remove strings before carving. Serves 6.

DEVILLED BEEF BONES

6 lbs. short ribs of beef or lamb or pork riblets
1 Tb. instant meat tenderizer
2 qts. water
2 large onions, quartered
2 tsp. salt
1 bay leaf
1 tsp. pepper

DEVIL'S SAUCE:
1 cup tomato catsup
½ cup prepared mustard
½ cup finely chopped onion
¼ cup prepared horseradish, drained
2 garlic cloves, crushed
1 Tb. Worcestershire sauce
1 tsp. hot pepper sauce

Moisten 6 lbs. short ribs of beef (or lamb or pork riblets) with water and sprinkle with 1 tablespoon instant meat tenderizer. Pierce meat all over with a sharp-tined fork. Place short ribs in a large saucepan with 2 qts. water, 2 large onions, quartered, 2 teaspoons salt, 1 bay leaf and 1 teaspoon pepper. Bring to a boil, reduce heat, cover and simmer 40 to 45 minutes.

Devil's Sauce: Combine in a small bowl 1 cup tomato catsup, ½ cup each prepared mustard and finely chopped onion, ¼ cup prepared horseradish, drained, 2 garlic cloves, crushed, 1 tablespoon Worcestershire sauce and 1 teaspoon hot pepper sauce. Set aside.

Remove short ribs from saucepan when cooked and drain well. Place in a foil-lined shallow baking pan and brush well with hot sauce. Roast 30 minutes at 425°, brushing with sauce every 5 minutes. Serves 6.

STEAK NEPTUNE

LOBSTER TAILS:
6 (4-oz.) lobster tails
¼ cup softened butter or margarine
1 garlic clove, crushed
½ tsp. salt
¼ tsp. pepper
Paprika

STEAK:
6 slices eye round of beef, 1 inch thick
2 Tb. instant meat tenderizer
Hickory-smoked salt
2 Tb. olive oil or cooking oil

Lobster Tails: If 6 (4-oz.) lobster tails are frozen, defrost them. Cut away membranes on underside of each tail and loosen meat from shell, but do not remove. Bend lobster tails backwards until shell cracks.

To ¼ cup softened butter or margarine, add 1 garlic clove, crushed, ½ teaspoon salt and ¼ teaspoon pepper. Mix well. Spread on lobster meat. Broil 4 inches from source of heat, meat side up, 8 to 10 minutes. Turn shell side up and broil 8 to 10 minutes more. Sprinkle with paprika just before serving. Serves 6.

Steak: Tie each of 6 slices eye round of beef, 1 inch thick, with strong, white string to make 6 steaks. Moisten steaks on each side with water and sprinkle both sides of each steak with some of 2 tablespoons instant meat tenderizer. Prick steaks thoroughly on each side with a sharp-tined fork. Sprinkle top of each steak lightly with hickory-smoked salt.

In a large, heavy skillet, heat 2 tablespoons olive oil (or cooking oil) until sizzling. Place steaks, salted side down, in oil and pan-broil 5 to 6 minutes. Sprinkle lightly with hickory-smoked salt and turn. Pan-broil 5 to 6 minutes longer. Serves 6.

❋ *Note:* Pan-broil steaks 5 to 6 minutes per side for rare; 7 to 8 minutes per side for medium; 9 to 10 minutes per side for well done. This is good with quick parslied rice, made by stirring ⅓ cup chopped parsley into 3 cups cooked quick-cooking rice.

VERMONT BEEF BRISKET

1 (4-lb.) piece beef brisket
1 Tb. instant meat tenderizer
2 cups water
2 cups coarsely chopped onion
1 cup chopped celery leaves
1 bay leaf
1 Tb. salt
1 tsp. pepper
2 cups soft bread crumbs
¼ cup prepared mustard
¼ cup maple blended syrup
¼ tsp. powdered cloves

Moisten 1 (4-lb.) piece beef brisket on both sides with water and sprinkle each side with half the 1 tablespoon instant meat tenderizer. Pierce meat all over with sharp-tined fork. Place meat in a heavy skillet or Dutch oven and add 2 cups each water and coarsely chopped onion, 1 cup chopped celery leaves, 1 bay leaf, 1 tablespoon salt and 1 teaspoon pepper. Bring to a boil, reduce heat, cover and simmer 2 hours until meat is tender. Combine 2 cups soft bread crumbs, ¼ cup each prepared mustard and maple blended syrup, and ¼ teaspoon powdered cloves.

Remove meat from Dutch oven and drain well. Spread top of meat with crumb mixture and broil 6 inches from source of heat 5 minutes. Serve hot or cold. Serves 6 to 8.

❋ *Note:* This is an excellent buffet dish as it is easy to slice and arrange attractively and is delicious hot or cold.

BEEF WELLINGTON

1 (4-lb.) piece eye round of beef
1 Tb. instant meat tenderizer
½ lb. softened liverwurst
2 Tb. bourbon
½ cup chopped mushrooms
2 (10-oz.) pkgs. frozen puff pastry shells, defrosted
1 egg yolk
1 Tb. heavy cream

Moisten 1 (4-lb.) piece eye round of beef all over with water and sprinkle with 1 tablespoon instant meat tenderizer. Prick well with a sharp-tined fork and roast 40 minutes at 450°. Remove from oven and cool completely.

Mash ½ lb. liverwurst. Add 2 tablespoons bourbon and mix well. Stir in ½ cup chopped mushrooms. The mixture should be spreadable. If not, add 1 tablespoon cream. Spread liverwurst mixture over entire cooled beef. On a floured board, roll 2 (10-oz.) pkgs. frozen puff pastry shells, defrosted, into an oblong shape about ¼-inch thick. Wrap pastry around beef; trim dough and reserve trimmings. Moisten edges of pastry and enclose beef, pressing dough together to seal.

Cut fancy shapes from pastry trimmings and arrange over pastry-encased beef, first moistening backs of shapes with cold water. Brush decorated pastry with 1 egg yolk beaten with 1 tablespoon heavy cream and bake 30 minutes at 425°. Serves 6 to 8.

MEAT ROASTING CHART

Meat	Oven Temp.	Time per lb.	Internal Temp.*	Special Tips
Beef	325	20-30 mins.	140-170	Lower temp. is for rare, higher temp. is for well-done.
Chicken/ Capon	325	30 mins.	—	As with all poultry, drumstick should pull away easily when done.
Duck	425 for ½ hour, then reduce to 375.	30 mins.	185	Prick skin of duck or goose before roasting to drain off surplus fat.
Turkey	325	30 mins.	185	Cover breast with butter-soaked cheese cloth during first half of cooking time.
Goose	325	30-40 mins.	185	For crispy skin, roast 30 mins. at 400 then reduce to 325.
Ham (Fully Cooked)	325	20-30 mins.	130	—
Lamb	375	20-30 mins.	160-180	Lower temp. is for "pink" meat, higher temp. is for well-done.
Pork	325	25-35 mins.	185	Score surface fat well in diamond shapes and rub seasonings in surface.
Veal	325	25-30 mins.	170	Baste frequently or cover with bacon strips while roasting.

*Use meat thermometer. Insert away from bone, in fleshy part of meat.

CHAPTER FOUR / VEGETABLES

The best vegetable, of course, is that which is lovingly bought and carefully prepared. No amount of sauce can hide improper cooking, but (big but) . . . you'll be surprised how *dazzling* vegetables can be, with but a few quick and simple flourishes. Like broccoli, served in a buttery sauce studded with salty toasted pecans. Or pumpkin, transformed into fritters. Or Belgian endive, cooked and served with a ham and tongue sauce that has its origins in gypsy cookery. Vegetables, in short, that are all dressed up with *someplace* to go . . .

SWEET AND SOUR BEETS

2 Tb. cornstarch
½ cup orange juice
½ cup lemon juice
¼ cup sugar
¼ cup butter or margarine
1 tsp. grated orange rind
1 tsp. grated lemon rind
½ tsp. salt
¼ tsp. pepper
4 cups cooked julienne beets (2 lbs. whole beets or 2 [16-oz.] cans julienne beets, drained)

In top of double boiler, blend 2 tablespoons cornstarch with ½ cup each orange juice and lemon juice until smooth. Place over direct heat and stir constantly until sauce is thickened.

Remove from heat and add ¼ cup each sugar and butter or margarine, 1 teaspoon each grated orange rind and grated lemon rind, ½ teaspoon salt and ¼ teaspoon pepper. Stir until sugar dissolves and butter is well blended.

Stir in 4 cups cooked julienne beets and heat over low heat until beets are piping hot. (Or place over hot water to reheat, and to keep hot until serving time.) Serves 6 to 8.

❉ Note: To cook whole beets, cut stalk to 2 inches in length. Wash. Do not peel or remove root. Cook, covered, in boiling salted water until just tender—about 30 to 45 minutes. Cool. Remove stalk, root and skin and cut in julienne strips.

STIR-FRIED ASPARAGUS

2 ½ to 3 lbs. fresh young asparagus
½ cup butter or margarine
½ cup olive oil or salad oil
¼ cup lemon juice
2 tsp. coarse-crystal salt
½ tsp. coarsely ground black pepper

Remove leafy tips from stalks of 2½ to 3 lbs. fresh young asparagus (do not peel with parer and do not remove tops). Cut on the diagonal in 1-inch strips. Wash very well to remove sand, drain and pat dry.

In a large skillet, heat ¼ cup of the butter or margarine and ¼ cup olive oil (or salad oil) until sizzling. Add half the asparagus and cook 2 to 3 minutes over high heat, stirring gently but constantly. When tender yet still crisp, remove with slotted spoon and drain on paper towels. Keep warm.

Repeat, using remaining ¼ cup butter or margarine and olive oil (or salad oil) and asparagus. Sprinkle cooked asparagus with ¼ cup lemon juice, 2 teaspoons coarse-crystal salt and ½ teaspoon coarsely ground black pepper and serve immediately. Serves 6 to 8.

❋ *Note:* To use frozen asparagus, you'll need 2 (10-oz.) pkgs. frozen asparagus spears, thawed. Drain and pat very dry with paper towels. Cut on diagonal in 1-inch strips. Sauté 1 pkg. at a time, using only a *total* of ¼ cup each butter or margarine and oil. Season as directed above.

GREEN BEANS SUPREME

2 lbs. whole green beans or 2 (10-oz.) pkgs. frozen whole green beans
2 cups sliced mushrooms (2 lbs.)
½ cup chopped onion
1 garlic clove, crushed
2 Tb. butter or margarine
¾ cup sour cream
1 tsp. salt
¼ tsp. pepper
½ cup fresh bread crumbs
¼ cup grated Parmesan cheese

Snip both ends from 2 lbs. whole green beans and cook in boiling salted water until *just* tender—about 3 to 5 minutes. (Or cook 2 [10-oz.] pkgs. frozen whole green beans according to directions, but for only half the cooking time.) Drain well.
In a skillet, sauté 2 cups sliced mushrooms, ½ cup chopped onion and 1 garlic clove, crushed, in 2 tablespoons butter or margarine until tender. Stir into drained beans, together with ¾ cup sour cream, 1 teaspoon salt and ¼ teaspoon pepper. Turn into a 2-qt. casserole and sprinkle top with a mixture of ½ cup fresh bread crumbs and ¼ cup grated Parmesan cheese. Bake 20 to 25 minutes at 350°, or until top is bubbly and golden. Serves 6 to 8.

AVOCADO AND CORN

2 (10-oz.) pkgs. frozen kernel corn
1 cup finely sliced celery
¼ cup lemon juice
2 Tb. olive or salad oil
½ tsp. hot pepper sauce
2 cups diced avocado

Cook 2 (10-oz.) pkgs. frozen kernel corn according to label directions, adding 1 cup finely sliced celery. Drain and heat gently in ¼ cup lemon juice, 2 tablespoons olive or salad oil, and ½ teaspoon hot pepper sauce. Remove from heat. Fold in 2 cups diced avocado and let stand, covered, 5-10 minutes or until avocado is heated through. Serves 6.

AVOCADO RICE

¾ cup chopped celery
¾ cup chopped onion
3 garlic cloves, crushed
¼ cup butter or margarine
2 cups water or chicken broth
2 cups quick-cooking rice
1 ½ tsp. salt
¼ tsp. pepper
2 cups coarsely diced avocado (1 large avocado)
¼ cup lemon juice

In a large saucepan, sauté ¾ cup each chopped celery and chopped onion and 3 garlic cloves, crushed, in ¼ cup butter or margarine until golden and tender—about 10 minutes. Add 2 cups water (or chicken broth) and bring quickly to a boil. Stir in 2 cups quick-cooking rice, 1 ½ teaspoons salt and ¼ teaspoon pepper.

Remove pan from heat and gently stir in 2 cups coarsely diced avocado which has been tossed in ¼ cup lemon juice. Cover pan and set aside 5 minutes for rice to absorb liquid and to allow avocado dice to heat through. Serves 6 to 8.

BEAN SPROUTS ORIENTALE

½ cup chopped onion
2 Tb. salad oil
1 (16-oz.) can bean sprouts, rinsed and drained
1 (6-oz.) can water chestnuts, drained and sliced
¼ cup chopped parsley
1 tsp. salt

In a skillet sauté ½ cup chopped onion in 2 tablespoons salad oil until golden. Turn heat to high and add 1 (16-oz.) can bean sprouts, rinsed and drained, and 1 (6-oz.) can water chestnuts, drained and sliced. Cook for 3 minutes, stirring constantly, until vegetables are heated through. Remove from heat. Sprinkle ¼ cup chopped parsley and 1 teaspoon salt over bean sprouts. Toss well to combine and serve immediately. Serves 6.

BAKED ACORN SQUASH

4 medium-sized, firm acorn squash
1 ½ tsp. salt
½ tsp. pepper
½ cup butter or margarine
¼ cup tawny port
¼ cup maple blended syrup
1 (14-oz.) jar cranberry-orange relish (about 1 ½ cups)

Wash and dry 4 medium-sized, firm acorn squash and cut in half lengthwise. Place squash halves on a shallow baking pan. Rub into the flesh of each a little of 1 ½ teaspoons salt and ½ teaspoon pepper.

In center cavity of each, place 1 tablespoon butter or margarine (using ½ cup in all) and 1 ½ teaspoons each tawny port and maple blended syrup (using ¼ cup each altogether). Cover squash halves loosely with foil and pour a little hot water into baking pan. Bake 30 to 40 minutes at 375°, or until tender.

Combine any cooking liquid from center of squash halves with 1 (14-oz.) jar cranberry-orange relish. Heat and stir to mix well. Fill each half with 2 tablespooons cranberry-orange relish and serve the remaining relish alongside. Serves 6 to 8.

Spinach-Stuffed Squash Variation: Prepare and bake 4 medium-sized squash as directed in recipe above, using same seasonings. Prepare stuffing by placing 1 lb. torn spinach, well washed and dried, in a large skillet together with 2 cups coarsely diced tomatoes and 2 cloves garlic, crushed. Cook, covered, over medium heat until spinach is limp but has not lost texture (about 2-3 minutes). Stir in any cooking liquid from center of squash. Divide spinach-tomato mixture between squash. Serves 6 to 8.

BROCCOLI WITH TOASTED SALTED PECANS

1 large bunch fresh broccoli or 2 (10-oz.) pkgs. frozen broccoli spears
2 Tb. cornstarch
½ cup chicken broth
½ cup lemon juice
1 Tb. sugar
1 ½ tsp. grated lemon rind
¼ tsp. salt
¼ tsp. pepper
½ cup pecan halves
1 Tb. butter or margarine
1 tsp. salt

Wash, trim and cut 1 large bunch fresh broccoli into spears. Place in 1 inch boiling salted water and cook, covered, over medium heat 8 to 10 minutes, or until tender. (Or prepare 2 [10-oz.] pkgs. frozen broccoli spears according to directions.) Drain well and place attractively on serving platter. Keep warm. Meanwhile, make a lemon sauce by blending 2 tablespoons cornstarch with ½ cup each chicken broth and lemon juice. Bring to a boil and cook, stirring constantly, until thickened. Stir in 1 tablespoon sugar, 1 ½ teaspoons grated lemon rind and ¼ teaspoon each salt and pepper.

Pour sauce over broccoli. Top with ½ cup pecan halves, which have been sautéed in 1 tablespoon butter or margarine and sprinkled with 1 teaspoon salt. Serves 6 to 8.

BRUSSELS SPROUTS WITH CHESTNUT SAUCE

½ lb. fresh chestnuts
2 Tb. butter or margarine, melted
2 cups beef broth
1 garlic clove, crushed
1 tsp. salt
¼ tsp. pepper
¼ tsp. nutmeg

4 cups (1 qt.) Brussels sprouts or 2 (10-oz.) pkgs. frozen Brussels sprouts
¼ cup chopped parsley

Chestnut Sauce: Make a cross on flat side of ½ lb. fresh chestnuts. Toss in 2 tablespoons butter or margarine, melted, and bake about 20 minutes at 350°, until shells curl back. Peel shells while hot and discard. Soak peeled chestnuts in hot water 5 minutes; then peel off bitter brown inner skin.

In a small saucepan, simmer prepared chestnuts, covered, with 2 cups beef broth, 1 garlic clove, crushed, and 1 teaspoon salt until tender—about 20 minutes. Press entire mixture through a sieve. Beat in 1 additional tablespoon butter or margarine and ¼ teaspoon each pepper and nutmeg. (Add more beef broth if chestnut puree is not the proper consistency to coat Brussels sprouts.) Keep warm.

Prepare 4 cups Brussels sprouts by trimming base and removing discolored outer leaves. Rinse well in cold water. Cook, covered, in 1 inch boiling, salted water 6 to 8 minutes. (Or prepare 2 [10-oz.] pkgs. frozen Brussels sprouts according to label directions.) Drain well. Toss gently with hot Chestnut Sauce and ¼ cup chopped parsley. Serves 6 to 8.

❋ *Note:* Fresh chestnuts are at their best during the holiday season. They take a little while to prepare, but they're well worth the trouble.

BUTTERY BAKED CARROTS

2 lbs. fresh carrots
½ cup maple blended syrup
½ cup butter or margarine, melted
2 tsp. salt
½ tsp. pepper
½ tsp. cinnamon

Wash, peel and coarsely grate 2 lbs. fresh carrots, to measure 8 cups. Place in a 2½- to 3-qt. casserole, tossing gently to combine with ½ cup each maple blended syrup and butter or margarine, melted, 2 teaspoons salt and ½ teaspoon each pepper and cinnamon. Bake, covered, 20 to 30 minutes at 350°, or until carrots are tender. Stir before serving. Serves 6 to 8.

❊ *Note:* White turnips, rutabaga or parsnips provide ideal alternates to the carrots in this delicious recipe.

CABBAGE AND CREAM

1 large head firm green cabbage
1 cup water
1 ½ tsp. salt
½ cup heavy cream
2 Tb. grated onion
½ tsp. pepper
½ tsp. nutmeg
1 cup grated, sharp Cheddar cheese

Shred fine 1 large head firm green cabbage to measure 8 to 10 cups. Cook, covered, in a large saucepan containing 1 cup boiling water and 1 ½ teaspoons salt, until tender-crisp—about 4 to 5 minutes. Drain well and return to saucepan. Add ½ cup heavy cream, 2 tablespoons grated onion and ½ teaspoon each pepper and nutmeg. Heat very slowly, tossing to mix well. Toss in 1 cup grated, sharp Cheddar cheese and stir to melt cheese. Serve at once. Serves 6 to 8.

COLCANNON

1 head firm green cabbage
1 cup water
4 cups hot mashed potatoes
½ cup finely chopped scallions
¼ cup heavy cream
¼ cup butter or margarine
1 ½ tsp. salt
½ tsp. freshly ground black pepper
¼ tsp. nutmeg
2 Tb. butter or margarine

Shred fine 1 head firm green cabbage, to measure 8 cups. Cook, covered, until tender-crisp in 1 cup boiling salted water. Drain well. Blend, beating vigorously, with 4 cups hot mashed potatoes. Beat in ½ cup finely chopped scallions, ¼ cup each heavy cream and butter or margarine, 1 ½ teaspoons salt, ½ teaspoon ground black pepper and ¼ teaspoon nutmeg. Mound in a heat-proof casserole. Dot with 2 tablespoons additional butter or margarine and broil until bubbly and golden, about 6 inches from source of heat. Serves 6 to 8.

❋ Note: Cook 4 large potatoes, peeled, to make 4 cups mashed, or save time by using instant mashed potatoes, prepared according to label directions.
For variety, beat ¾ cup grated, sharp Cheddar cheese into cabbage-potato mixture. Broil as directed, sprinkling with ¼ cup additional grated cheese as well as dotting with butter or margarine.

POTATO SOUFFLÉ

5 eggs
¼ cup butter or margarine
¼ cup all-purpose flour
1 ½ cups milk
¼ cup grated, sharp Cheddar cheese
2 garlic cloves, crushed
1 ½ tsp. salt
¼ tsp. pepper
1 ½ cups cold mashed potatoes
¼ tsp. cream of tartar

Allow 5 eggs to come to room temperature, then separate. In a large saucepan, melt ¼ cup butter or margarine. Blend in ¼ cup all-purpose flour and heat 30 seconds. Blend in 1 ½ cups milk and cook, stirring, over low heat, until sauce is thickened and smooth. Remove from heat.

Beat in egg yolks, ¼ cup grated, sharp Cheddar cheese, 2 garlic cloves, crushed, 1 ½ teaspoons salt and ¼ teaspoon pepper. Evenly blend in 1 ½ cups of cold mashed potatoes.

In a separate bowl, beat egg whites at high speed with ¼ teaspoon cream of tartar until they form stiff peaks. Gently fold into potato mixture, using a wire whisk or spatula. Turn into a greased, 2-qt. soufflé dish with a foil collar extending 3 inches above rim of dish. Bake 45 to 50 minutes at 375° and serve at once. Serves 6 to 8.

✳ *Note:* Leftover cold mashed potatoes can be used here. Or re-constitute 1 cup instant mashed potatoes using 1 cup water and ¼ cup milk. Cool before using.

You may use 1 ½ cups cold mashed sweet potatoes, if you wish, instead of the regular potatoes, for an interesting variation.

RED CABBAGE NORMAND

2 Tb. butter or margarine
¾ cup chopped onion
1 firm head red cabbage
¾ cup raspberry jam or strawberry jam
¾ cup wine vinegar
¾ cup water
¼ cup brown sugar
2 tsp. salt
¼ tsp. pepper
4 cups sliced, peeled, tart apples

Melt 2 tablespoons butter or margarine in a large saucepan and sauté ¾ cup chopped onion until transparent. Coarsely shred 1 firm head red cabbage, to measure 8 cups. Add cabbage to onion, along with ¾ cup each raspberry jam (or strawberry jam), wine vinegar and water, ¼ cup brown sugar, 2 teaspoons salt and ¼ teaspoon pepper.
Simmer, covered, 45 minutes. Add 4 cups sliced, peeled, tart apples and toss gently to combine with cabbage. Simmer, covered, 15 minutes more. Serve with pan juices. Serves 6 to 8.

BATTER-FRIED ZUCCHINI

4 cups sliced (¼ -inch) zucchini
1 cup unsifted flour
Batter:
1 cup milk
1 cup unsifted flour
2 eggs
1 ½ tsp. salt
½ tsp. pepper
1 cup dry seasoned bread crumbs
1 qt. salad oil

Place 4 cups sliced zucchini in ice water. Cover and refrigerate until serving time. Drain and dry; toss with 1 cup unsifted flour to coat. Make batter by combining 1 cup each milk and unsifted flour. Add 2 eggs, slightly beaten, 1 ½ teaspoons salt and ½ teaspoon pepper. Stir until smooth. Place floured zucchini slices, a few at a time, in batter. Toss in 1 cup dry bread crumbs. Fry in 1 qt. salad oil heated to 375°, cooking ½ cup at a time. Serves 6.

PUMPKIN FRITTERS

3 Tb. butter or margarine
3 Tb. flour
1 cup milk
2 eggs, separated
1 cup pumpkin puree
2 Tb. grated onion
1 tsp. salt
½ tsp. baking powder
¼ tsp. pepper
¼ tsp. nutmeg
Cooking oil

In a medium saucepan, melt 3 tablespoons butter or margarine. Stir in 3 tablespoons flour and heat 30 seconds. Blend in 1 cup milk and bring to a boil. Cook, stirring, until thickened. Remove from heat and blend in 2 egg yolks, 1 cup pumpkin puree, 2 tablespoons grated onion, 1 teaspoon salt, ½ teaspoon baking powder and ¼ teaspoon each pepper and nutmeg.
In a small bowl, beat 2 egg whites. Gently fold into pumpkin mixture. Drop by heaping tablespoons onto a lightly oiled griddle or skillet, frying no more than 4 at a time about 2 minutes per side. Makes about 24. Serves 6 to 8.

❋ *Note:* When to serve these tasty little fritters? With leftover cold turkey or ham—perfect.
The following vegetables may be substituted for the pumpkin puree and the fritters can be enjoyed in a variety of tastes. Use 1 cup mashed potatoes or mashed sweet potatoes, finely chopped, well drained, cooked spinach, or finely chopped fresh mushrooms, finely chopped onions or finely grated carrot, pressed free of moisture.

CORN PUFFLE

1 Tb. flour
2 garlic cloves, crushed
1 ½ tsp. dry mustard
1 ½ tsp. Worcestershire sauce
½ tsp. salt
5 eggs, separated
1 (10 ¾ -oz.) can Cheddar cheese soup
4 ears fresh corn
⅛ tsp. cream of tartar

In a large saucepan, blend 1 tablespoon flour, 2 garlic cloves, crushed, 1 ½ teaspoons each dry mustard and Worcestershire sauce and ½ teaspoon salt. Stir in 5 egg yolks (place egg whites in large bowl and let stand at room temperature). Blend in 1 (10¾-oz.) can Cheddar cheese soup. Cook over low heat, stirring, until mixture is thick and comes to a gentle simmer. Remove from heat and cool 10 minutes.

Cook 4 ears fresh corn in boiling salted water 5 minutes. Drain well. Cut kernels from cobs with a sharp knife, to measure 2 cups. Stir into cheese mixture.

Add ⅛ teaspoon cream of tartar to egg whites. Beat at high speed until stiff, firm peaks form, then fold into cooled cheese mixture. Pour into a 2-qt. soufflé dish with a 3-inch foil collar extending above rim of dish. Bake 40 minutes at 400° and serve at once. Serves 6 to 8.

❄ Note: If you wish, substitute 1 (10-oz.) pkg. frozen cut corn, thawed and well-drained (not cooked) for the fresh corn.

RATATOUILLE

2 cups (½ -inch) eggplant cubes (1 medium-sized eggplant, peeled)
3 garlic cloves, crushed
⅓ cup olive oil
1 ½ teaspoons salt
2 cups thinly sliced onion
1 cup green pepper strips
1 cup sweet red pepper strips
2 cups tomato slices (2 large tomatoes)
½ tsp. basil

Place 2 cups (½-inch) eggplant cubes over bottom of a 2½-qt. casserole. Sprinkle 1 of the garlic cloves, crushed, 2 tablespoons of the olive oil and ½ teaspoon of the salt over eggplant. Top with 2 cups thinly sliced onion.

Sprinkle onions with second clove garlic, crushed, 2 tablespoons olive oil and ½ teaspoon salt and top with a layer of 1 cup each green pepper strips and sweet red pepper strips. Sprinkle with remaining 1 garlic clove, crushed, the remaining olive oil and ½ teaspoon salt. Bake, covered, 45 minutes at 350°.

Remove cover. Arrange 2 cups tomato slices over top. Baste with a little of the cooking liquor and sprinkle with ½ teaspoon basil. Continue baking, uncovered, 15 minutes more. Serve hot or cold. Serves 6 to 8. (See photograph.)

❋ Note: Ratatouille can be cooked, covered, on top of stove over low heat for 45 minutes. Add tomatoes. Cook, covered, 5 minutes more. Then uncover and cook 10 minutes longer to reduce cooking liquid.

Very unclassic . . . but 1 ½ lbs. ground beef can be sautéed and layered into the casserole to make this a main dish. Cook as directed above.

BELGIAN ENDIVE WITH ZINGARA SAUCE

8 to 10 firm heads Belgian endive
¼ cup butter or margarine
¼ cup lemon juice
1 (10 ½ -oz.) can chicken broth
½ tsp. salt

ZINGARA SAUCE:
2 Tb. cornstarch
2 cups reserved cooking liquid
½ cup julienne strips cooked tongue
½ cup julienne strips cooked ham
½ tsp. salt
¼ tsp. pepper
¼ tsp. liquid gravy seasoning

Wash 8 to 10 firm heads Belgian endive and discard any imperfect outer leaves. Dry well. In a large skillet, melt ¼ cup butter or margarine. Stir in ¼ cup lemon juice and add endive. Toss gently to coat evenly with lemon-butter. Add 1 (10½-oz.) can chicken broth and ½ teaspoon salt. Cover tightly and simmer gently 20 to 30 minutes, or until endive is tender. Drain well, reserving cooking liquid. Arrange endive on serving platter and keep warm.

Zingara Sauce: Blend 2 tablespoons cornstarch with 2 cups reserved cooking liquid (add dry sherry or port if necessary to make up 2 cups). Bring to a boil, stirring constantly. Add ½ cup each julienne strips cooked tongue and cooked ham, ½ teaspoon salt and ¼ teaspoon each pepper and liquid gravy seasoning. Simmer 2 to 3 minutes to heat meat. Pour over endive. Serves 6 to 8.

✳ Note: If fresh endive is unavailable, use 2 (16-oz.) cans, drained. Heat only 5 minutes in cooking liquid, then proceed as directed. "Zingara" is the German word for gypsy—and this is a marvelously exotic sauce. (See photograph.)

KOHLRABI SMITANE

2 ½ lbs. kohlrabi
¼ cup butter or margarine
½ cup sour cream
1 Tb. horseradish, drained
1 ½ tsp. salt
¼ tsp. pepper
¼ tsp. nutmeg
¼ cup chopped parsley

Remove root and stem ends from 2½ lbs. kohlrabi. Peel and grate on coarse side of grater, to make 6 to 8 cups.

In a medium saucepan, melt ¼ cup butter or margarine. Add grated kohlrabi and toss well. Cover and place on low heat, and toss frequently. Kohlrabi will cook in butter and its own juices in about 5 to 7 minutes.

Stir in ½ cup sour cream, 1 tablespoon horseradish, drained, 1 ½ teaspoons salt and ¼ teaspoon each pepper and nutmeg. Heat gently until very hot, but do *not* boil. Stir in ¼ cup chopped parsley (or sprinkle over top) just before serving. Serves 6 to 8.

✳ *Note:* Kohlrabi, a relative of cabbage, is actually a turnip "bulb" from which grow slender stalks with cabbage-like leaves on top. If the leaves are still young and tender they can be used as a separate vegetable. Grated white turnip or carrot may be substituted for kohlrabi.

ONIONS DANISH-STYLE

2 ½ lbs. fresh silverskin onions
¾ cup granulated sugar
⅓ cup butter or margarine
¼ cup chopped parsley
1 ½ tsp. freshly ground black pepper

Peel 2½ lbs. fresh silverskin onions. Cut a small slit in the root end of each and cook, covered, in boiling salted water until just tender. Drain well and pat dry on paper towels. Cool. In a large skillet, slowly melt ¾ cup granulated sugar, stirring constantly, over low heat. (Sugar must not become too dark.) Add onions. Turn so all sides become evenly golden. Add ⅓ cup butter or margarine, ¼ cup chopped parsley and 1 ½ teaspoons freshly ground black pepper. Toss gently.

Remove onions from skillet. Pour any sauce remaining in skillet over onions and serve at once. Serves 6 to 8.

❊ Note: Canned silverskins won't work in this recipe as they are too moist.

CELERY AMANDINE

6 cups diced celery
¾ cup butter or margarine
¾ cup chopped scallions
¼ cup snipped chives or 2 Tb. dried chives
1 garlic clove, crushed
1 tsp. salt
¼ tsp. pepper
1 cup blanched, slivered almonds

In a heavy skillet, sauté 6 cups diced celery in ½ cup of the butter or margarine. Cook, stirring constantly, 4 to 5 minutes, until celery is tender-crisp. Add ¾ cup chopped scallions, ¼ cup snipped chives (or 2 tablespoons dried chives), 1 garlic clove, crushed, 1 teaspoon salt and ¼ teaspoon pepper. Stir 2 to 3 minutes more. Celery should still be tender-crisp.

In a small skillet, sauté 1 cup blanched, slivered almonds in remaining ¼ cup butter or margarine. Stir almonds and browned butter into celery and serve at once. Serves 6 to 8.

SESAME SPINACH

2 ½ lbs. young spinach (3 [10-oz.] bags)
½ cup sesame seeds
2 Tb. olive oil
2 Tb. butter or margarine
¼ cup tarragon vinegar or cider vinegar
1 ½ tsp. salt
½ tsp. pepper

Wash 2½ lbs. young spinach leaves and drain very well. Tear any large leaves into bite-sized pieces.

In a large skillet, sauté ½ cup sesame seeds in 2 tablespoons each olive oil and butter or margarine until pale gold. Add drained spinach and cook 2 minutes, stirring constantly. Add ¼ cup tarragon vinegar (or cider vinegar), 1 ½ teaspoons salt and ½ teaspoon pepper. Toss to mix well and serve at once. Serves 6 to 8.

❀ *Note:* Frozen leaf spinach won't work here. Sorry . . . it's too moist.

OVEN-CRISPED CARROTS

3 cups pared carrots in 1-inch pieces
¼ cup butter or margarine
½ cup crushed bran flakes
½ cup flaked coconut
½ cup very finely chopped pecans
1 Tb. light brown sugar
¼ tsp. ground coriander or nutmeg

Cook 3 cups pared carrots in 1-inch pieces in lightly salted water, simmering for 15 minutes or until just tender. Drain. Add ¼ cup butter or margarine. Toss until butter melts and carrots are well coated. Let cool 5 minutes. Preheat oven to 350°.

In a large plastic bag place ½ cup each crushed bran flakes, flaked coconut and very finely chopped pecans, 1 tablespoon light brown sugar and ¼ teaspoon ground coriander (or nutmeg). Shake to mix. Add carrots, shaking to coat well.

Place in large shallow baking pan. Bake at 350° for 20 minutes or until coconut is lightly toasted. Serves 6.

CHAPTER FIVE / WELCOME WINTER SALADS

Salad: can be a first course, can be served with the main course, can be offered (with cheese) 'twixt entrée and dessert, can stand on its own. Salad is all of these *and* a particularly welcome change of pace in winter. Some of the salads that follow complement a meal, others (the Beef Vinaigrette or Crab Louis, for instance) are a meal. Many use fresh produce that is readily available from October through January. All have a proper place on your holiday table.

AVOCADO AND GRAPEFRUIT SALAD

3 grapefruit
2 ripe avocados
Chicory
¾ cup olive oil or salad oil
¼ cup tarragon vinegar
1 tsp. sugar
½ tsp. salt
½ tsp. dry mustard
¼ tsp. ginger
¼ tsp. pepper

Peel and section 3 grapefruit, placing any surplus juice in a small bowl. Peel and slice 2 ripe avocados, dipping each slice into grapefruit juice to prevent discoloration. Arrange grapefruit sections and avocado slices on bed of chicory which has been washed and thoroughly dried.

Combine ¾ cup olive oil (or salad oil), ¼ cup tarragon vinegar, 1 teaspoon sugar, ½ teaspoon each salt and dry mustard and ¼ teaspoon each ginger and pepper. Mix well and serve over salad. Serves 6.

HEARTS OF PALM AND RADISH SALAD

1 (14-oz.) can hearts of palm, thinly sliced (about 2 cups)
2 cups thin radish slices
¼ cup chopped parsley
1 cup sour cream
2 Tb. lemon juice
1 Tb. drained, bottled horseradish
1 tsp. salt
Lettuce

Drain 1 (14-oz.) can hearts of palm and slice contents thin. Combine with 2 cups thin radish slices and ¼ cup chopped parsley and toss lightly. Combine 1 cup sour cream, 2 tablespoons lemon juice, 1 tablespoon drained, bottled horseradish and 1 teaspoon salt, mixing well. Add to palm and radish mixture and stir gently. Chill. Serve on lettuce leaves. Serves 6.

GREEK SALAD

2 cups tiny raw cauliflowerettes
2 cups thinly sliced, raw mushrooms
2 cups sliced, pitted black olives
1 cup diced green pepper (½ -inch dice)
1 (8-oz.) carton plain yogurt
½ cup olive oil
¼ cup chopped parsley
1 garlic clove, crushed
1 tsp. salt
½ tsp. pepper
Lettuce

Combine in a large bowl 2 cups tiny raw cauliflowerettes, 2 cups each thinly sliced, raw mushrooms and sliced, pitted black olives and 1 cup diced green pepper. Toss lightly to mix.
Combine 1 (8-oz.) carton plain yogurt, ½ cup olive oil, ¼ cup chopped parsley, 1 garlic clove, crushed, 1 teaspoon salt and ½ teaspoon pepper. Mix well and pour over raw vegetables. Serve salad on lettuce leaves. Serves 6.

OKRA AND OYSTER SALAD

2 (10-oz.) pkgs. frozen okra, cooked and drained
1 cup bottled oil and garlic dressing
¼ cup chopped parsley
½ tsp. hot pepper sauce
2 (8-oz.) cans whole oysters, drained
1 cup sliced unpeeled cucumber
Lettuce

While still hot, blend 2 (10-oz.) pkgs. frozen okra, cooked and drained, with 1 cup bottled oil and garlic dressing, ¼ cup chopped parsley and ½ tsp. hot pepper sauce. Cool and chill at least 1 hour. Add 2 (8-oz.) cans whole oysters, drained, and 1 cup sliced unpeeled cucumber. Chill 30 minutes more. Drain from dressing. Serve on lettuce leaves in a large bowl or on individual platters. Serves 6.

CAESAR SALAD

2 heads Romaine lettuce (8 cups)
2 (2-oz.) cans flat anchovies
¼ lb. blue cheese, finely crumbled
½ cup garlic-flavored croutons
½ cup grated Parmesan cheese
1 Tb. capers, drained
2 egg yolks
2 Tb. lemon juice
1 cup olive oil
¼ cup vinegar
1 tsp. salt
¼ tsp. pepper

Separate leaves of 2 heads Romaine lettuce. Wash, drain and dry well. Roll lightly in paper towels and chill.

Break lettuce leaves into bite-sized pieces and place in a large salad bowl. Drain 2 (2-oz.) cans flat anchovies and cut each filet into 4 pieces. Scatter anchovies over top of salad, along with ¼ lb. blue cheese, finely crumbled, ½ cup each garlic-flavored croutons and grated Parmesan cheese and 1 tablespoon capers, drained. Toss well.

Combine 2 egg yolks with 2 tablespoons lemon juice, 1 cup olive oil, ¼ cup vinegar, 1 teaspoon salt and ¼ teaspoon pepper. Toss well and serve at once. Serves 6 to 8.

✻ Note: You could use 8 cups mixed salad greens instead of Romaine only. Use 2 or more of the following—Boston, iceberg or Bibb lettuce, chicory, endive, escarole, dandelion greens or spinach leaves. If you want to use bottled Caesar salad dressing, blend 1 cup with egg yolks and lemon juice and omit the olive oil, vinegar, salt and pepper called for above.

To make a spectacular of this salad, mix it at the table. Here's how: Arrange salad greens in a bowl and bring to the table set on a large, round platter on which are nicely arranged the anchovies, blue cheese, capers, croutons, Parmesan cheese, egg yolks (each in half a shell, if possible), a halved lemon cut in 4 wedges and the dressing ingredients, mixed.

Add anchovies, blue cheese, capers and croutons to lettuce and toss well. Then add whole egg yolks, lemon juice and mixed dressing. Toss *thoroughly* and serve.

How to make garlic-flavored croutons? Remove crusts from 1 slice thin-sliced bread and cut into ¼-inch dice. Heat 2 table-spoons butter or margarine with 1 split garlic clove until butter sizzles. Add bread cubes and sauté, tossing often, until they are crisp and golden. Drain well. Makes ½ cup.

GERMAN POTATO SALAD

8 cups sliced potatoes (about 3 lbs.)
2 tsp. salt
8 slices bacon, cut into 1-inch pieces
1 cup chopped onion
1 small garlic clove, crushed
¾ cup cider vinegar
2 Tb. sugar
½ tsp. pepper

Pare about 3 lbs. potatoes and cut into ¼-inch-thick slices, to make 8 cups. Place in a saucepan, cover with cold water, add 2 teaspoons salt and bring to a boil. Cover and cook 10 to 15 minutes, or until potato slices are just tender. Drain well.

Cook 8 slices bacon, cut into 1-inch pieces, until crisp. Remove from skillet and set aside. Pour off all but about ¼ cup bacon fat and add to skillet 1 cup chopped onion and 1 small garlic clove, crushed. Cook, stirring, 2 or 3 minutes. Add ¾ cup cider vinegar, 2 tablespoons sugar and ½ teaspoon pepper, stirring to blend. Pour over hot, cooked potato slices, toss gently and serve. Serves 6.

SPINACH AND BACON SALAD

1 lb. young spinach
6 slices bacon
1 garlic clove, crushed
4 slices bread, cubed
½ cup olive oil
2 Tb. lemon juice
½ tsp. sugar
¼ tsp. dry mustard
¼ tsp. salt
⅛ tsp. pepper

Remove stems from 1 lb. young spinach, wash leaves and dry thoroughly. Shred coarsely. Fry 6 slices bacon until crisp, drain well and crumble. Set aside. In fat remaining in skillet, sauté 1 garlic clove, crushed, and 4 slices bread, cubed. When "croutons" are crisp-brown, drain on paper towels. Set aside. Combine ½ cup olive oil, 2 tablespoons lemon juice, ½ teaspoon sugar, ¼ teaspoon each dry mustard and salt and ⅛ teaspoon pepper. Mix well and pour over dried spinach greens in serving bowl. Toss to coat greens. Top salad with crumbled bacon and croutons. Toss again just before serving. Serves 6.

❋ Note: This may be served hot, too. Prepare spinach as for cold version, then combine lemon juice and seasonings, omitting olive oil. Set aside. Sauté bacon, drain and crumble. Sauté garlic and bread cubes and drain. To remaining bacon fat, add lemon juice and seasonings, bring quickly to a boil and pour over shredded spinach. Top with bacon and croutons and toss well. Serve immediately.

BEEF VINAIGRETTE

6 cups julienne strips cold, cooked beef
1 cup thinly sliced onion rings
1 cup olive oil
¼ cup tarragon vinegar
1 garlic clove, cut in half
1 tsp. salt
½ tsp. basil, crushed
¼ tsp. pepper
6 leaves iceberg lettuce
2 Tb. chopped parsley

Combine 6 cups julienne strips cold, cooked beef (cut to measure about ¼ x ¼ x ½-inch), 1 cup each thinly sliced onion rings and olive oil, ¼ cup tarragon vinegar, 1 garlic clove, cut in half, 1 teaspoon salt, ½ teaspoon basil, crushed, and ¼ teaspoon pepper. Toss to mix well, cover and let stand at room temperature 1 hour. Chill 2 hours, tossing occasionally. Wash thoroughly 6 leaves iceberg lettuce. Wrap in paper towels and chill. Just before serving, line bowl with lettuce leaves. Spoon beef salad (from which garlic has been removed) into center of lettuce and sprinkle with 2 tablespoons chopped parsley. Serves 6.

✻ Note: This ideal way of using leftover holiday roast beef can be prepared in the evening and chilled overnight. Arrange on lettuce just before serving.

MACARONI SALAD

4 cups elbow macaroni
3 qts. boiling water
1 Tb. salt
1 cup coarsely shredded carrots
1 cup sliced scallions
¼ cup drained capers
1 cup mayonnaise
½ cup sour cream
Lettuce

Cook 4 cups elbow macaroni in 3 qts. boiling water with 1 tablespoon salt 10 to 15 minutes, or until macaroni is tender. Drain and rinse with cold water. Drain again and cool.
Combine cooked macaroni, 1 cup each coarsely shredded carrots and sliced scallions and ¼ cup drained capers. Mix 1 cup mayonnaise with ½ cup sour cream and add to macaroni mixture. Stir gently to mix well. Chill. Serve on lettuce. Serves 6.

ARTICHOKE, SHRIMP AND RICE SALAD

1 ½ lbs. cooked small shrimp or 4 (4 ½-oz.) cans shrimp, drained
2 (9-oz.) pkgs. frozen artichoke hearts or 1 (14-oz.) can artichoke
   hearts, drained
1 ½ cups quick-cooking rice (3 cups, cooked)
½ cup sliced scallions
½ cup bottled garlic French dressing
Watercress

Combine 1 ½ lbs. cooked small shrimp (or 4 [4½-oz.] cans shrimp, drained) and 2 (9-oz.) pkgs. frozen artichoke hearts, prepared according to directions (or 1 [14-oz.] can artichoke hearts, drained).
Cook 1 ½ cups quick-cooking rice according to directions and add to shrimp mixture, along with ½ cup sliced scallions and ½ cup bottled garlic French dressing. Toss to mix well. Chill 30 minutes. Serve garnished with watercress. Serves 6.

Orange and
Onion Salad

Mexican
Salad

WALDORF SALAD

6 red-skinned apples
1 cup chopped celery
1 cup coarsely chopped walnuts
1 cup mayonnaise
2 Tb. lemon juice
6 lettuce cups

Wash, dry and polish 6 red-skinned apples. Cut in quarters and core each quarter but do not peel. Cut each quarter into ½-inch cubes and place in a medium bowl. Add 1 cup each chopped celery and coarsely chopped walnuts. Toss lightly. Combine 1 cup mayonnaise with 2 tablespoons lemon juice and stir. Add to apple mixture and stir lightly to mix well. Serve in 6 individual lettuce "cups". Serves 6.

❋ Note: The Waldorf Astoria Hotel, from whence this salad originates, now uses pecans as well as, or in place of, walnuts. If they can, you can!

PEAR SALAD WITH O'HENRY'S DRESSING

6 ripe pears, chilled
6 cups shredded lettuce
1 cup sour cream
¼ cup crumbled blue cheese
Fresh nutmeg

Cut 6 ripe pears, chilled, in quarters. Core and cut each quarter in half lengthwise. On 6 individual salad plates, arrange 1 cup shredded lettuce and 8 pear slices. To 1 cup sour cream, add ¼ cup crumbled blue cheese and mix well. Place a dollop of dressing on each salad and sprinkle lightly with a grating of fresh nutmeg. Serves 6.

❋ Note: Bottled blue cheese dressing may be substituted for the sour cream and crumbled blue cheese, if you wish. O'Henry's dressing, by the way, is simply blue cheese crumbled into sour cream.

CRAB LOUIS

2 heads Boston lettuce
3 (6-oz.) pkgs. frozen, cooked crabmeat, defrosted, or 3 cups fresh or
    canned crabmeat
4 hard-cooked eggs, chopped
4 tomatoes, each cut into 6 wedges
1 cup mayonnaise
½ cup heavy cream, whipped
½ cup catsup
¼ cup chopped green pepper
¼ cup chopped scallions

Separate lettuce leaves from 2 heads Boston lettuce, wash, pat
dry and roll lightly in paper towels. Chill.

Arrange lettuce on a large, round serving plate and place
3 (6-oz.) pkgs. frozen, cooked crabmeat, defrosted (or 3 cups
fresh or canned crabmeat) in center. Form a ring of chopped,
hard-cooked eggs (using 4) around crabmeat, then arrange 4
tomatoes, each cut into 6 wedges, on lettuce.

Serve with Louis dressing made by combining 1 cup mayonnaise
with ½ cup each heavy cream, whipped, and catsup and ¼ cup
each chopped green pepper and chopped scallions. Serves 6.

❊ Note: A magnificent salad from the West Coast to feature
Pacific crabmeat. However, debate rages as to the exact recipe.
Some versions do not permit tomatoes, some sprinkle the salad
with chives, and some spike the Louis dressing with 2 tablepoons
chili sauce and ½ teaspoon Worcestershire to make a hotter
sea food sauce.

THREE-BEAN SALAD WITH CERVELAT

1 cup dried lima beans
1 cup dried navy beans
1 cup dried kidney beans
1 cup olive oil
¼ cup cider vinegar
2 to 4 garlic cloves, crushed
1 cup chopped parsley
2 tsp. salt
½ tsp. pepper
¼ lb. cervelat, thinly sliced
Lettuce leaves

Cook 1 cup each dried lima beans, dried navy beans and dried kidney beans according to label directions. Drain well and place all beans in a large bowl. While hot, pour a dressing over them made by combining the following ingredients: Combine 1 cup olive oil, ¼ cup cider vinegar, 2 to 4 garlic cloves, crushed, 1 cup chopped parsley, 2 teaspoons salt and ½ teaspoon pepper. Toss lightly with hot beans to mix well and let stand at room temperature at least 30 minutes. Chill. Just before serving, add ¼ lb. cervelat, thinly sliced. Mix again, gently. Serve on lettuce leaves. Serves 6.

❄ *Note:* A more expensive but quicker version of this can be made by using well drained canned beans or frozen beans, cooked, or a combination of both. Thin slices of salami, cut in quarters, or thin slices of pepperoni, frankfurters, knockwurst or bologna could also be used, instead of cervelat.

ENDIVE AND PINEAPPLE SALAD

6 heads Belgian endive
4 cups drained, canned pineapple chunks (2 [20-oz.] cans)
1 cup mayonnaise
½ cup pineapple juice
2 Tb. chopped parsley
1 cup coconut, toasted
1 tsp. salt

Trim ends of 6 heads Belgian endive, and remove and discard any coarse outer leaves. Cut each trimmed head into ½-inch slices and add to 4 cups canned pineapple chunks, well drained (reserve juice). Toss to mix thoroughly. Combine 1 cup mayonnaise, ½ cup reserved pineapple juice and 2 tablespoons chopped parsley. Spoon over individual servings of endive and pineapple mixture. Sprinkle some of 1 cup coconut, salted and toasted, over top. Serves 6.

❋ *Note:* Not sure how to prepare coconut? Spread 1 cup flaked coconut on a baking sheet and sprinkle with 1 teaspoon salt. Toast 10 to 12 minutes at 325°, or until golden.

SALAD JOHANNES

12 canned peach halves, well drained (2 [1 lb. 13-oz.] cans)
Salad greens
¼ cup finely chopped, crystallized ginger
1 cup sour cream
2 Tb. maple blended syrup
2 Tb. lemon juice
2 Tb. brandy

Drain 12 canned peach halves thoroughly. Arrange on salad greens and spoon 1 teaspoon of the ¼ cup finely chopped, crystallized ginger into hollow of each peach. Serve topped with dressing made by combining 1 cup sour cream with 2 tablespoons each maple blended syrup, lemon juice and brandy, stirring to mix well. Serves 6.

CHRISTMAS SLAW

6 cups shredded green cabbage (½ medium head)
6 cups shredded red cabbage (½ medium head)
½ cup chopped onion
1 cup sour cream
½ cup mayonnaise
¼ cup tarragon vinegar
2 tsp. salt
1 tsp. celery seed

Toss well together 6 cups each shredded green cabbage and shredded red cabbage and ½ cup chopped onion. Combine 1 cup sour cream, ½ cup mayonnaise, ¼ cup tarragon vinegar, 2 teaspoons salt and 1 teaspoon celery seed. Add to cabbage and onion and toss to mix thoroughly. Serves 6.

HERRING AND POTATO SALAD

1 (12-oz.) jar marinated herring and onions in wine sauce
6 cups peeled, sliced potatoes (about 2 lbs.)
1 cup sliced celery
½ cup white wine
¼ cup olive oil
¼ cup chopped onion
2 Tb. chopped fresh dill or 1 tsp. dried dill
2 Tb. chopped parsley
Lettuce

Drain 1 (12-oz.) jar marinated herring and onions in wine sauce and cut herring into bite-sized pieces. Set aside.

Place 6 cups peeled, sliced potatoes in boiling salted water to cover and boil 10 to 15 minutes, or until tender. Drain. Place hot potatoes in a large bowl and add 1 cup sliced celery, ½ cup white wine and ¼ cup each olive oil and chopped onion, 2 tablespoons each chopped fresh dill (or 1 teaspoon dried dill) and chopped parsley.

Carefully stir to mix well. Cover and let stand at room temperature until potatoes are cooled. Stir in drained herring and chill, covered. Serve in a lettuce-lined bowl. Serves 6 to 8.

MEXICAN SALAD

2 cups raw zucchini slices (about ½ lb.)
1 (10-oz.) pkg. frozen corn, cooked
1 cup roasted sweet red pepper strips (a 7-oz. jar)
¾ cup olive oil
¼ cup cider vinegar
2 tsp. salt
1 garlic clove, crushed
1 tsp. sugar
1 tsp. curry powder
Lettuce "cups"

In a bowl, combine 2 cups raw zucchini slices, 1 (10-oz.) pkg. frozen corn, cooked, and 1 cup roasted sweet red pepper strips. Combine ¾ cup olive oil, ¼ cup cider vinegar, 2 teaspoons salt, 1 garlic clove, crushed, 1 teaspoon each sugar and curry powder. Pour over vegetables and mix. Let stand at room temperature 1 hour to blend flavors. Cover and chill.

Just before serving, drain well, reserving the dressing. Serve in lettuce "cups" with the reserved dressing alongside. Serves 6.

❉ *Note:* Substitute 2 cups fresh, cooked corn for the frozen, or a 16-oz. can kernel corn, drained. Jars of sweet red peppers are available in most markets. *(See photograph.)*

Make a variation on Mexican Salad by using the same dresssing and marinating 1 hour, at room temperature, 2 cups cooked garbanzos (chick peas) and 1 cup each diced avocado and sliced black olives. Cover and chill. Add ½ cup toasted slivered almonds. Drain and serve as above.

HEARTS OF LETTUCE AND TOMATO

1 large firm head iceberg lettuce
3 tomatoes
¾ cup olive oil
¼ cup tarragon vinegar
1 tsp. dried basil, crumbled
½ tsp. sugar
½ tsp. salt
¼ tsp. pepper

Remove coarse outer leaves and core of 1 large, firm head iceberg lettuce. Wash and drain well. Wrap in paper towels and chill until ready to use.
Cut lettuce head in 6 wedges. Cut each of 3 tomatoes in 6 wedges. On individual salad plates, arrange 1 lettuce wedge and 3 tomato wedges. Combine ¾ cup olive oil, ¼ cup tarragon vinegar, 1 teaspoon dried basil, crumbled, ½ teaspoon each sugar and salt and ¼ teaspoon pepper. Pour over salad and serve. Serves 6.

ORANGE AND ONION SALAD

3 large oranges
1 large onion
1 cup heavy cream
1 tsp. salt
¼ cup maple blended syrup
Boston lettuce or Watercress

Peel 3 large oranges. Remove all white pith. Slice each orange into 6 slices. Peel 1 large onion. Cut in 12 very thin slices. Whip 1 cup heavy cream with 1 teaspoon salt until cream is very stiff. Stir in ¼ cup maple blended syrup. Arrange 3 orange slices and 2 onion slices on individual salad plates and surround with Boston lettuce or watercress. Spoon a ribbon of maple cream dressing over each salad. Serves 6.

❋ *Note:* Or arrange salad in one large bowl *(see photograph)*, serving dressing alongside.

CHAPTER SIX / CONFECTIONS & COOKIES

Who among us is not enticed by the spicy-sweet aroma of cookies in the oven, or tugged nostalgically by the fun of a taffy pull? For many, mere mention of the holidays conjures up heady visions of sweet candies and cookies: the urge to go quickly to the kitchen to brew up something marvelous becomes too strong to resist. We have recipes to satisfy the most ambitious or the most casual longings for something sinfully sweet. All bespeak affection when presented as a small holiday gift, and (need we say?) are excellent to have on hand for holiday visitors.

CANDY

SNOWY DAY FUDGE

1 ⅔ cups sugar
⅔ cup evaporated milk
1 (6-oz.) pkg. semi-sweet chocolate chips
1 ½ cups miniature marshmallows
½ cup quartered candied cherries
½ cup whole blanched pistachio nuts

In a medium saucepan, combine 1 ⅔ cups sugar with ⅔ cup evaporated milk and cook over medium heat, stirring constantly, until sugar is dissolved and mixture comes to a boil.
Boil, stirring, 5 minutes. Remove from heat and stir in 1 (6-oz.) pkg. semi-sweet chocolate chips and 1 ½ cups miniature marshmallows. When chocolate and marshmallows are melted, stir in ½ cup quartered candied cherries and ½ cup whole blanched pistachio nuts. Stir until thickened and pour into a greased 8x8x2-inch pan; cool. Cut into 1-inch squares. Makes about 5 dozen pieces.

❊ Note: This is a fool-proof recipe which will work, no matter what the weather.

TURKISH DELIGHT

6 (3-oz.) pkgs. raspberry-flavored gelatine
2 cups boiling water
1 Tb. fresh lemon or lime juice
Confectioners sugar

Place 6 (3-oz.) pkgs. raspberry-flavored gelatine in a medium saucepan and add 2 cups boiling water. Stir to dissolve thoroughly. Bring to a simmer over low heat and cook 5 minutes. Remove from heat and stir in 1 tablespoon fresh lemon (or lime) juice. Rinse an 8x8x2-inch pan in cold water and do not dry. Pour hot gelatine into pan. Cool and chill until firm. Cut into 1-inch squares. Toss in confectioners sugar. Makes 5 dozen.

ALMOND CALISSONS

1 (8-oz.) can almond paste
1 lb. confectioners sugar, sifted
1 egg white
1 Tb. maple blended syrup
8 to 10 drops red food color
¼ cup chopped candied cherries
½ cup chopped toasted almonds

Place 1 (8-oz.) can almond paste in a large bowl with 1 lb. confectioners sugar, sifted, 1 egg white and 1 tablespoon maple blended syrup. Knead mixture until it becomes smooth and pliable. Add 8 to 10 drops red food color and knead well into this marzipan mixture. The color should be pale pink.
Knead ¼ cup chopped candied cherries into marzipan, and then ½ cup chopped toasted almonds. Divide into 8 equal portions. Form each portion into a ¼-inch-thick roll. Cut each roll into 2-inch lengths. Makes about 16½ dozen pieces.

GINGER-STUFFED DATES

12 pitted dates
1 Tb. crème de menthe
6 marshmallows
1 Tb. chopped crystallized ginger

Press open 12 pitted dates and pour a little of 1 tablespoon crème de menthe into each. Set aside. Cut 6 marshmallows in half. In center of each half place a little of 1 tablespoon chopped crystallized ginger. Fold marshmallow over ginger and tuck stuffed marshmallows into prepared date. Makes 1 dozen.

SESAME SEED BRITTLE

1 cup sesame seeds
1 Tb. butter or margarine
2 cups sugar
1 cup water
¼ cup light corn syrup

Stir 1 cup sesame seeds in 1 tablespoon butter or margarine in a medium skillet until seeds are golden. Turn onto paper towels to drain and cool.

Combine 2 cups sugar, 1 cup water and ¼ cup light corn syrup in a medium saucepan and cook, stirring, until sugar dissolves. Allow to cook without stirring until temperature reaches 238° on candy thermometer (or until syrup forms a soft ball when a small amount is dropped in very cold water).

Gently stir in the toasted sesame seeds and continue cooking until temperature is 270° on candy thermometer (or until syrup forms a hard but not brittle thread when a little is dropped in cold water). Immediately pour onto a well-greased baking pan. When cold, crack into bite-sized pieces. Makes about ¾ lb.

MOCK MARZIPAN

2 cups sifted confectioners sugar
¼ cup cold mashed potatoes
1 (8-oz.) can blanched almonds
1 egg white
1 Tb. fresh lemon juice
½ tsp. almond extract

Mix 2 cups sifted confectioners sugar with ¼ cup cold mashed potatoes. Place contents of 1 (8-oz.) can blanched almonds in blender container and whir until almonds are very fine. Add to potato mixture along with 1 egg white, 1 tablespoon fresh lemon juice and ½ teaspoon almond extract. Knead with hands until mixture is workable, adding a few more drops lemon juice, if necessary, to make mixture pliable.

Shape "marzipan" into fruits, flowers, leaves, etc., and paint with water-diluted food colorings. Allow to dry. Makes 1 lb.

❄ *Note:* Instant mashed potatoes will *not* work in this recipe.

OLD-FASHIONED MOLASSES TAFFY

1 ¼ cups dark molasses
1 cup sugar
1 Tb. cider vinegar
2 Tb. butter or margarine

Combine 1 ¼ cups dark molasses, 1 cup sugar and 1 tablespoon cider vinegar in a medium saucepan. Cook, stirring constantly, over low heat until sugar dissolves. Continue cooking, without stirring, until mixture comes to a boil. Boil until temperature reads 270° on candy thermometer (or until syrup forms brittle threads when a small amount is dropped into very cold water). Stir syrup gently 3 or 4 times during the boiling period.
Remove from heat at once and stir in 2 tablespoons butter or margarine. Pour taffy onto a well-greased shallow pan and let stand until just cool enough to touch, or until a finger pressed into it makes a dent.
With lightly greased hands, gather taffy into a ball. Pull until it is pale golden. Roll into long, thin ropes and cut each rope into 1-inch pieces. Work quickly at this point. Makes ¾ lb.

❋ *Note:* To make Molasses Peppermint Taffy, add ½ teaspoon peppermint extract (or 3 to 4 drops oil of peppermint) when you add the butter or margarine.
Taffy may also be pulled into flat ribbons before cutting, to make good, old fashioned ribbon taffy. Or, pull it into ropes as above, cut into ½-inch pieces and twist each piece, to make what are known as "Humbugs".

PEANUT BUTTER CRISPS

½ cup butter or margarine
½ cup milk
2 cups sugar
¼ cup unsweetened cocoa
¼ cup peanut butter
½ tsp. salt
2 cups quick-cooking oats
½ cup chopped peanuts

Melt ½ cup butter or margarine in a saucepan. Add ½ cup milk, 2 cups sugar, ¼ cup unsweetened cocoa and cook, stirring, until sugar dissolves. Bring to a boil for 3 minutes.
Remove from heat and immediately add ¼ cup peanut butter and ½ teaspoon salt; stir to blend. Add 2 cups quick-cooking oats and mix well. Drop by teaspoons onto waxed paper and sprinkle with ½ cup chopped peanuts. Or, mixture could be dropped by teaspoons into tiny fluted candy paper. Makes about 4 dozen.

PENUCHE

¼ cup butter or margarine
½ cup firmly packed light brown sugar
½ cup dried milk powder
½ cup dark corn syrup
1 Tb. cold water
1 tsp. vanilla extract
4 cups sifted confectioners sugar
1 cup chopped pecans

In top of double boiler, over hot (not boiling) water, melt ¼ cup butter or margarine. Stir in ½ cup firmly packed light brown sugar, ½ cup each dried milk powder and dark corn syrup, 1 tablespoon cold water and 1 teaspoon vanilla extract.
Add 3 cups sifted confectioners sugar and beat vigorously with a wooden spoon. Add remaining 1 cup sifted confectioners sugar and beat well. Remove from heat and stir in 1 cup chopped pecans. Pour into a lightly greased 8x8x2-inch pan. Cool, then cut into 1-inch squares. Makes about 5 dozen.

APRICOT-COCONUT SQUARES

¼ lb. marshmallows
2 Tb. light corn syrup
2 Tb. butter or margarine
2 Tb. water
2 cups chopped, dried apricots
1 cup shredded coconut
1 cup chopped walnuts
1 cup dried milk powder
½ cup confectioners sugar

In top of double boiler, combine ¼ lb. marshmallows and 2 tablespoons each light corn syrup, butter or margarine and water. Cover and heat over hot water until marshmallows and butter or margarine are melted. Remove from heat and stir.

In a large bowl, combine 2 cups chopped, dried apricots, 1 cup each shredded coconut, walnuts and dried milk powder and ½ cup confectioners sugar. Stir into marshmallow mixture and blend thoroughly.

Press into a greased 8x8x2-inch square pan, or drop by teaspoons into tiny fluted candy papers. Makes about 5 dozen.

STUFFED KUMQUATS

1 (12½-oz.) jar kumquats, drained
½ (8-oz.) can almond paste

Drain 1 (12½-oz.) jar kumquats very well. Cut each (there should be about 24) into 4 petals about ¾ way down. Remove centers. Using 1 teaspoon almond paste for each, form 24 oval-shaped nuggets. Stuff each kumquat with nugget of almond paste. Chill. Makes 1¼ lbs.

COOKIES

ITALIAN ALMOND KISSES

1 (8-oz.) can almond paste
1 cup sugar
2 egg whites
¼ cup sifted flour
¼ cup confectioners sugar
½ cup finely chopped, mixed candied fruit
½ cup slivered blanched almonds

Combine 1 (8-oz.) can almond paste, 1 cup sugar and 2 egg whites in a medium bowl and work together with fingers to form a smooth paste. Still kneading, work in ¼ cup sifted flour, then ¼ cup confectioners sugar. Finally knead in ½ cup finely chopped, mixed candied fruit.
Drop mixture by teaspoons onto a lightly greased baking sheet, placing cookies 2 inches apart. Poke a few pieces of the ½ cup slivered blanched almonds into top of each cookie. Bake 20 to 25 minutes at 300°. Remove from cookie sheet immediately and cool on wire racks. Makes about 4 dozen.

CHRISTMAS MACAROONS

¼ cup butter or margarine
½ lb. marshmallows (32 large mashmallows)
2 Tb. maple blended syrup
4 cups cornflakes
½ cup chopped, toasted almonds
½ cup mixed candied fruit

In top of double boiler, over hot (not boiling) water, melt ¼ cup butter or margarine and ½ lb. marshmallows. Add 2 tablespoons maple blended syrup and stir to mix well.
Combine 4 cups cornflakes and ½ cup each chopped, toasted almonds and mixed candied fruit. Pour hot marshmallow mixture over almond and fruit mixture and toss lightly with a fork to mix thoroughly. Drop by teaspoons onto waxed paper. Let cool. Makes about 3 dozen.

Irish
Mince Pies

Spritz
Wreaths

Edelweiss
Cookies

Orange
Bavarian

Cranberries
in Snow

Queen of
Puddings

TYROLEAN SPRINGERLI

1 cup cooking oil
1 cup sugar
2 eggs
1 tsp. anise flavoring
4 cups sifted flour
1 Tb. baking powder
1 tsp. salt
1 egg yolk
1 Tb. heavy cream
¼ cup chopped hazelnuts

Combine 1 cup each cooking oil and sugar, 2 eggs and 1 teaspoon anise flavoring. Beat until smooth. Mix 4 cups sifted flour with 1 tablespoon baking powder and 1 teaspoon salt. Add 3 cups of this flour mixture to oil, sugar and eggs. Mix well.

Add remaining 1 cup flour mixture and work dough with hands. Divide in half. Wrap each half in plastic wrap, foil or waxed paper and chill at least 1 hour.

Place half the dough on a lightly floured surface and roll out to a 10-inch square. Cut into 2-inch squares and place on an ungreased baking sheet.

Combine and mix well 1 egg yolk and 1 tablespoon heavy cream and brush top of each square lightly with a small amount of this mixture. (Save some for the second dough half.) Top each cookie with a few of the ¼ cup chopped hazelnuts (reserving some for other half of dough). Bake 15 minutes at 350°; remove from pan and cool on wire racks. Repeat with second half of dough.

Store baked cookies in a covered container or covered with plastic wrap or foil for 12 hours before serving. Makes 4 dozen.

IRISH MINCE PIES

1 (10-oz.) pkg. frozen puff pastry shells, defrosted
1 ½ cups prepared mincemeat

Roll out each puff pastry shell, defrosted, (1 [10-oz.] pkg.) into a 6-inch square. With a 3-inch cookie cutter, cut each square into 4 (3-inch) circles. Fit circles into small cupcake tins and prick each with a fork.

Place 1 tablespoon prepared mincemeat in each prepared pastry shell. Bake 20 minutes at 400°. Remove from baking tins and serve warm or cooled. Top with whipped cream or hard sauce if desired. Makes 24. (See photograph.)

DUTCH YULE COOKIES

2 cups sifted cake flour
1 tsp. cinnamon
1 tsp. salt
½ tsp. nutmeg
¼ tsp. ginger
⅛ tsp. pepper
½ cup dark molasses
¼ cup firmly packed dark brown sugar
¼ cup melted butter or margarine

Combine 2 cups sifted cake flour with 1 teaspoon each cinnamon and salt, ½ teaspoon nutmeg, ¼ teaspoon ginger and ⅛ teaspoon pepper. Stir gently to mix well.

Combine ½ cup dark molasses, ¼ cup each firmly packed dark brown sugar and melted butter or margarine. Add to flour mixture and mix well. Wrap dough in plastic wrap, foil or waxed paper and chill at least 1 hour.

Using ¼ of the dough at a time, roll out ⅛ inch thick on a lightly floured surface. Cut with a 1 ½-inch round cookie cutter. Place on a lightly greased cookie sheet and bake 10 minutes at 350°. Remove to wire rack and cool. Makes about 8 dozen cookies.

LEBKUCHEN

2 ¼ cups sifted flour
1 tsp. salt
1 tsp. baking powder
1 tsp. allspice
1 tsp. cinnamon
3 egg yolks
1 ½ cups firmly packed dark brown sugar
2 tsp. powdered instant coffee
½ cup water
1 cup chopped hazelnuts or walnuts

BUTTERCREAM FROSTING:
½ cup softened butter or margarine
2 cups confectioners sugar
1 egg white
1 tsp. vanilla extract

In a medium bowl, combine 2¼ cups sifted flour and 1 teaspoon each salt, baking powder, allspice and cinnamon. Beat 3 egg yolks with electric or rotary beater until thick and lemon colored. Gradually beat in 1½ cups firmly packed dark brown sugar. Stir in half the flour mixture.

Dissolve 2 teaspoons powdered instant coffee in ½ cup water. Add to batter and blend. Add remaining flour and mix well. Stir in 1 cup chopped hazelnuts (or walnuts). Turn into a greased 15x10x1-inch jelly roll pan and bake 25 minutes at 375°. Cool in pan then set on wire rack. Spread with frosting.

Buttercream Frosting: Cream ½ cup softened butter or margarine with 2 cups confectioners sugar. Add 1 egg white and 1 teaspoon vanilla extract and beat well with a wooden spoon until smooth and creamy. Spread over cake in pan and cut into 1x2-inch bars. Makes about 6 dozen.

EDELWEISS COOKIES

1 cup softened butter or margarine
½ cup firmly packed light brown sugar
1 tsp. vanilla extract
2 ½ cups sifted flour
½ tsp. salt
Blanched almonds, split
Cinnamon hots
1 egg yolk
1 Tb. milk

To 1 cup softened butter or margarine, add ½ cup firmly packed light brown sugar and 1 teaspoon vanilla extract. Beat until light and fluffy. Add 2½ cups sifted flour and ½ tsp. salt. Divide dough in half. Wrap in plastic wrap, foil or waxed paper.

Roll out half the dough ¼-inch thick on a lightly floured surface. Cut with a 2-inch fluted cookie cutter and place cookies 1 inch apart on a lightly greased cookie sheet. Arrange 5 blanched almond halves, petal-fashion, on each cookie, with a cinnamon hot in the center. Repeat with second half of dough. Beat 1 egg yolk with 1 tablespoon milk and brush some of this lightly over decorated cookie (reserving some for other half of dough). Bake 10 to 15 minutes at 325°, or until cookies and almonds are golden brown. Makes 5 dozen. (See photograph.)

❋ Note: To split blanched almonds, cover them with boiling water and let stand 5 minutes. Drain, split apart and let stand on paper towels to dry.

This recipe will also make traditional shortbread. Divide dough in half and press out each half into a 7-inch circle on a lightly greased cookie sheet. Flute the edges, then mark each circle in 8 wedges. Bake 30 minutes at 325° and cool on baking sheet. Do not decorate with almonds and candied cherries as in Edelweiss Cookies, and do not glaze.

MEXICAN FRUIT BARS

1 (6-oz.) pkg. butterscotch chips
½ cup butter or margarine
½ cup dark brown sugar
1 ½ cups flour
1 tsp. baking powder
½ tsp. salt
1 cup chopped, toasted almonds
½ cup mixed candied fruit
½ cup currants
2 eggs, slightly beaten
1 Tb. grated orange rind

In double boiler, over hot (not boiling) water, melt 1 (6-oz.) pkg. butterscotch chips and ½ cup butter or margarine with ½ cup dark brown sugar. Remove from heat. Stir to mix well.

Combine 1 ½ cups flour, 1 teaspoon baking powder and ½ teaspoon salt, stirring gently to blend. Stir into butterscotch mixture. Spread batter evenly in a greased 13x9x2-inch pan. Bake 20 minutes at 350° and remove from oven.

Meanwhile, combine 1 cup chopped, toasted almonds, ½ cup each mixed candied fruit and currants, 2 eggs, slightly beaten, and 1 tablespoon grated orange rind. Spread evenly over hot cookie dough. Return to oven and bake 20 minutes more at 350°. Cool in pan. Cut into 2x1-inch bars. Makes 4½ dozen.

SPRITZ WREATHS

1 cup softened butter or margarine
1 ¼ cups confectioners sugar
2 egg yolks
1 tsp. vanilla extract
½ tsp. salt
2 ½ cups flour
Candied cherries
Candied citron

To 1 cup softened butter or margarine, gradually add 1 ¼ cups confectioners sugar, beating until mixture is light and fluffy. Add 2 egg yolks, 1 teaspoon vanilla extract, ½ teaspoon salt, and beat again. Stir in 2½ cups flour and mix until dough is well blended and smooth.

Place dough in a pastry bag or tube with a large fluted tip, and press dough in 2½-inch circles onto an ungreased baking sheet. Decorate each circle with bits of candied cherries and citron. Bake 10 to 12 minutes at 375°, but do not allow to brown. Cool on baking sheet 2 minutes, then remove to wire rack. Makes about 3 dozen. *(See photograph.)*

✳ *Note:* Do not use packaged soft margarine in this recipe. Use regular margarine and allow to soften at room temperature (if you do not use butter).

ECCLES CAKES

1 (10-oz.) pkg. frozen puff pastry shells
¼ cup mincemeat
Granulated sugar

Defrost 1 (10-oz.) pkg. frozen puff pastry shells. Roll each one into a 4x8-inch oblong. Cut in half to form two 4x4-inch squares. Place 1 teaspoon mincemeat in center of each. Moisten edges of dough and fold over to enclose filling completely. Roll in granulated sugar. Cut three small diagonal slashes on surface of each. Place on ungreased baking sheet. Bake at 400° for 15 to 20 minutes. Makes 12.

CHOCOLATE-MAPLE BOURBON BALLS

½ cup maple blended syrup
1 (8 ½ -oz.) pkg. chocolate wafers, crushed
1 cup chopped walnuts
1 cup confectioners sugar
¼ cup bourbon
¼ cup sweetened cocoa mix

In a small saucepan, bring ½ cup maple blended syrup to a boil and boil gently until syrup is reduced to ¼ cup—about 3 to 4 minutes. Remove from heat and cool.
Combine 1 (8½-oz.) pkg. chocolate wafers, crushed, 1 cup each chopped walnuts and confectioners sugar, the reduced maple blended syrup and ¼ cup bourbon. Mix well and shape into balls, using 1 teaspoon per ball. Let stand 10 minutes, then roll in ¼ cup sweetened cocoa mix. Makes about 5 dozen.

SNOWBALL COOKIES

1 cup butter or margarine
⅓ cup confectioners sugar
1 tsp. vanilla extract
1 cup sifted all-purpose flour
1 cup chopped peanuts

Cream together 1 cup butter or margarine, ⅓ cup confectioners sugar and 1 teaspoon vanilla extract. Slowly blend in 1 cup each sifted all-purpose flour and chopped peanuts. Roll into cookies, using 2 teaspoons dough for each. Bake on lightly greased cookie sheet at 350° for 20 minutes. Cool on wire rack. Sprinkling with confectioners sugar. Makes 5 to 6 dozen.

CHAPTER SEVEN / BREADS AND CAKES

Settle back with a group of friends over a cup of hot tea, or a glass of eggnog, and a slice of something delicious . . . Panettone, Three Kings' Loaf or Gingerbread Stollen, for example. In this chapter are many such tempters—favorite breads and cakes (and a marvelous Pumpkin Pie) that will fill your house with the heady smell of spices and have your family and friends singing your praises. Many of these completed recipes benefit from well-wrapped storage, prior to eating, to allow the rich flavors to mingle. By the way, our fruit cake recipe has double value: with a few simple changes of procedure, it may be steamed, to make an admirable Christmas pudding.

GINGERBREAD STOLLEN

1 (13 ¾-oz.) pkg. hot roll mix
¾ cup warm water
1 egg, beaten
1 tsp. ginger
1 (14.5-oz.) pkg. gingerbread mix
½ cup water
1 cup golden raisins
1 cup mixed, candied fruit, chopped
2 Tb. rum

FROSTING:
¾ cup sifted confectioners sugar
1-1 ½ Tb. rum
¾ cup flaked or slivered almonds

Dissolve yeast contained in 1 (13¾-oz.) pkg. hot roll mix in ¾ cup warm water. Add 1 egg, beaten, the dry ingredients in hot roll mix and 1 teaspoon ginger. Blend thoroughly. Cover dough with damp cloth and allow to rise in a warm place 30 minutes, or until doubled in volume.

Prepare 1 (14.5-oz.) pkg. gingerbread mix according to label directions, using only ½ cup water. Add 1 cup each golden raisins and mixed, candied fruit, chopped, and 2 tablespoons rum.

Punch down hot roll dough and turn onto a floured surface. Knead 2 to 3 minutes, then roll out to a 15 x 12-inch rectangle. Spread gingerbread batter over hot roll dough, leaving a 1-inch margin along one 15-inch edge. Dampen this edge. Starting at the other 15-inch edge, roll up, jelly roll fashion, and press dampened edge to seal.

Lift roll onto a greased baking sheet. Make several slits 2 inches long and ½ inch deep across roll. Bake 40 to 45 minutes at 375°. Cool in pan 5 minutes, then lift to wire rack and cool completely.

To serve, make frosting by blending ¾ cup sifted confectioners sugar with 1-1½ tablespoons rum. Pour over Stollen. Sprinkle with ¾ cup flaked or slivered almonds. Serves 8 to 12.

PANETTONE

2 pkgs. dry active yeast
1 cup warm water
1 cup warm milk
3 eggs, beaten
¼ cup sugar
¼ cup softened butter or margarine
1 ½ tsp. salt
½ tsp. allspice
6 cups sifted all-purpose flour
1 cup chopped, mixed candied fruit
½ cup coarsely chopped golden raisins
½ cup chopped, blanched almonds

In a large bowl, blend 2 pkgs. dry active yeast and 1 cup warm water. Stir well to dissolve yeast, then beat in 1 cup warm milk, 3 eggs, beaten, ¼ cup each sugar and softened butter or margarine, 1 ½ teaspoons salt and ½ teaspoon allspice.

Gradually beat in 6 cups sifted all-purpose flour. Cover with damp cloth and let rise 30 minutes, until doubled in volume.

Mix into dough 1 cup chopped, mixed candied fruit and ½ cup each coarsely chopped golden raisins and chopped, blanched almonds. Spoon into 3 well-greased, 1-lb. coffee tins. Bake 45 minutes at 375°, or until a cake tester inserted down into center comes out clean. Coat in tins on wire racks for 5 minutes, then remove from tins to rack and cool completely.

To serve, cut horizontally through cake. Makes 3 cakes, to serve 15 to 20.

✽ Note: This is elegant with fresh fruit compotes, parfaits or cream desserts.

TRADITIONAL FRUIT CAKE

2 cups mixed, candied fruit
1 ½ cups coarsely broken walnuts
1 cup golden raisins
1 cup dark raisins
½ cup all-purpose flour
½ cup granulated sugar
½ cup light brown sugar, firmly packed
¼ cup softened butter or margarine
3 eggs
½ cup brandy or strong coffee
½ tsp. almond extract
1 cup sifted all-purpose flour
¼ tsp. allspice
¼ tsp. cinnamon
¼ tsp. baking soda

In a plastic or brown paper bag, combine 2 cups mixed, candied fruit, 1 ½ cups coarsely broken walnuts, 1 cup each golden raisins and dark raisins and ½ cup all-purpose flour. Toss to mix well and set aside.

In a large bowl, combine ½ cup each granulated sugar and light brown sugar, firmly packed, with ¼ cup softened butter or margarine. Beat until light and fluffy. Add 3 eggs, 1 at a time, beating well. Stir in ½ cup brandy (or strong coffee) and ½ teaspoon almond extract.

Sift together 1 cup sifted all-purpose flour with ¼ teaspoon each allspice, cinnamon and baking soda. Stir into sugar and egg mixture only until mixture is dampened. Add fruit and nut mixture to batter and mix thoroughly with a large spoon.

Prepare 1 (9-inch) spring form pan by oiling well and by lining the sides and base with oiled brown paper. Butter the oiled paper. Spoon batter into pan evenly. Bake 2½ hours at 275°, or until a cake tester comes out clean when inserted in center. Cool cake 1 hour in pan on wire rack. Remove pan, but not brown paper, and cool completely. Store wrapped in foil (remove paper at serving time). Serves 12 generously.

✳ Note: This same batter may be turned into a well-greased, 6-cup bowl or fluted mold, to make Christmas Pudding. Here's how: cover bowl with foil, and secure tightly, with string.

Place on trivet or wire rack in a large, deep saucepan or kettle. Fill saucepan half-full with boiling water, cover and simmer 2 hours, adding more boiling water if necessary. Cool completely. Add a new cover to bowl and store until needed. Reheat for 30 minutes in boiling water before serving.

Or, unmold and serve at once with whipped cream, or flamed with rum. Serves 6 to 8.

NORWEGIAN CHRISTMAS BREADS

1 (13 ¾-oz.) pkg. hot roll mix
¾ cup warm water
¼ cup chopped golden raisins
¼ cup chopped citron peel
1 tsp. grated lemon rind
1 tsp. ground cardamon
1 egg yolk
1 Tb. water

Prepare 1 (13¾-oz.) pkg. hot roll mix according to label directions, using ¾ cup warm water. Let rise, covered with a damp cloth, in a warm place 30 minutes, until doubled in volume.

Knead in ¼ cup each chopped golden raisins and chopped citron peel and 1 teaspoon each grated lemon rind and ground cardamon. Divide dough into 12 pieces. Knead each on a lightly floured board, then press into 12 (1½ x 2 x 3-inch) individual loaf pans. Cover and let rise 20 minutes in a warm place.

Brush top of each with glaze made by beating 1 egg yolk with 1 tablespoon water. Bake 25 to 30 minutes at 375°. Remove immediately from pans and cool on wire racks. Makes 12.

❋ Note: These are great to have on hand over the holidays— delicious with coffee, tea or eggnog. By the way, if you have no individual loaf pans, bake in very large muffin tins.

HUNGARIAN POPPY SEED CAKE

1 (19-oz.) pkg. yellow cake mix
1 (2 ⅛ -oz.) pkg. whipped topping mix
4 eggs
1 cup cold water
½ cup salad oil
½ cup poppy seeds

GLAZE:
1 orange rind, cut in julienne strips
1 lemon rind, cut in julienne strips
½ cup water
½ cup light corn syrup
2 Tb. lemon juice

In a medium bowl, combine 1 (19-oz.) pkg. yellow cake mix, 1 (2⅛-oz.) pkg. whipped topping mix, 4 eggs and 1 cup cold water. Beat at medium speed with electric beater 2 minutes, until batter is smooth. Add ½ cup each salad oil and poppy seeds and beat 2 minutes more.

Pour batter into a greased and floured 2½-qt. bundt pan (or 10-inch angel food cake pan). Bake 50 to 60 minutes at 350°; cool in pan on wire rack 25 minutes. Remove from pan and cool completely.

To make glaze: Simmer 1 orange rind, cut in julienne strips, and 1 lemon rind, cut in julienne strips, in ½ cup water 10 minutes. Drain, cool and set aside. Combine ½ cup light corn syrup with 2 tablespoons lemon juice. Boil until temperature reaches 238° on a candy thermometer (or until a small amount dropped in cold water forms a soft ball).

Brush all but about ¼ cup glaze over cake. Toss julienne strips of lemon and orange rind in reserved ¼ cup glaze and arrange in a decorative band around top of cake. Serves 10 to 12.

TRIPLE CHOCOLATE TORTE

1 (19-oz.) pkg. devil's food cake mix
2 eggs
1 ⅓ cups water
½ cup softened butter or margarine
½ cup heavy cream
1 (8-oz.) pkg. semi-sweet chocolate squares
6-8 cups sifted confectioners sugar (1 ½ lbs.)

Grease and flour 2 (9-inch) layer cake pans. Prepare 1 (19-oz.) pkg. devil's food cake mix according to label directions, using 2 eggs and 1 ⅓ cups water. Divide batter evenly between cake pans and bake 35 to 40 minutes at 350°, or until cake springs back when lightly touched with fingers. Cool 5 minutes in pans, then remove from pans and cool completely on wire racks.

In top of double boiler, over hot (not boiling) water, prepare frosting by beating together ½ cup each softened butter or margarine and heavy cream. Add all squares from 1 (8-oz.) pkg. semi-sweet chocolate. Allow chocolate to melt and beat in 6-8 cups sifted confectioners sugar. Cool only slightly.

Set 1 cake layer on serving plate. Top with ¾ cup frosting. Set second cake layer over first. Frost top and sides with remaining frosting. Let frosting cool completely before decorating.

To decorate, let additional squares semi-sweet chocolate soften at room temperature. Using a vegetable peeler, pare thin strips from chocolate to make curls. Cover top and sides of cake with chocolate curls and dust lightly with a little additional confectioners sugar. Serves 12.

APPLE-MARZIPAN KUCHEN

2 (10-oz.) pkgs. pie crust mix
½ cup cold water
2 (8-oz.) cans almond paste
½ lb. sesame seeds (2 cups)
¼ cup butter or margarine, melted
1 (22-oz.) can apple pie filling, drained
¼ cup apricot preserves, softened
1 egg yolk, beaten
1 Tb. cold water

Lightly oil a 9x5x3-inch loaf pan. Using a double thickness of foil, line the bottom and 2 longest sides of pan, making sure foil overhangs each side.

Prepare 2 (10-oz.) pkgs. pie crust mix according to label directions, using ½ cup cold water. Use ¾ of the dough, rolled out ¼ inch thick, to line bottom and sides of pan. Press dough firmly in place. Any seams of dough in corners of pan should be lightly moistened with water and sealed well. (Cover remaining pastry and set aside.)

Roll out 1 of the (8-oz.) cans almond paste to measure 9x5 inches and place in bottom of pastry-lined loaf pan.

In blender container, pulverize (a little at a time) ½ lb. sesame seeds. Blend all together with ¼ cup butter or margarine, melted. Divide mixture in half and spread one-half over almond paste. Top with half of 1 (22-oz.) can apple pie filling, drained as thoroughly as possible.

Roll out remaining (8-oz.) can almond paste to form a layer over apple pie filling. Top with remaining sesame seeds and apple pie filling. Brush apples with ¼ cup apricot preserves, softened.

Roll out remaining pastry and cut into ½-inch strips. Arrange strips in a lattice pattern over top of apples. Seal strips to edge of pastry by moistening with a little water. Flute edges and brush all over with a glaze made by combining well 1 egg yolk, beaten, with 1 tablespoon cold water.

Bake 45 minutes at 400°, until pastry is deep gold and crisp. Cool completely in pan on wire rack. Remove from pan, using over-hanging foil at sides. Serves 12.

GÖTEBURG LIMPA

1 (12-oz.) bottle or can light beer
2 pkgs. dry active yeast
1 cup warm milk
5 cups sifted rye or whole wheat flour
3 cups sifted all-purpose flour
2 cups light molasses
1 cup chopped walnuts
¼ cup grated orange rind

Boil 1 (12-oz.) bottle (or can) light beer 5 minutes. Let cool until just warm. Dissolve 2 pkgs. dry active yeast in 1 cup warm milk in a large bowl.

Blend together 5 cups sifted rye (or whole wheat) flour and 3 cups sifted all-purpose flour. Stir 1 cup flour into yeast mixture. Beat in cooled beer and 2 cups light molasses, adding remaining flour, 1 cup at a time, during this process. Stir in 1 cup chopped walnuts and ¼ cup grated orange rind. Cover bowl with damp cloth and let rise 45 to 60 minutes, until doubled in bulk.

Punch down dough and divide evenly between 2 (9x5x3-inch) loaf pans. Cover with damp cloth and let dough rise again until top is level with rim of pan.

Bake 1 to 1 ¼ hours at 375°, or until loaves sound hollow when tapped. Remove from pans and cool completely on wire rack before slicing. Makes 2 loaves.

❋ *Note:* In most supermarkets or health stores, you will easily find rye or whole wheat flour. This is a favorite sweet bread of the Swedes.

PUMPKIN PIE

1 (10-oz.) pkg. pie crust mix
¼ cup ice water
3 eggs
½ cup sugar
¼ cup dark molasses
1 tsp. ginger
1 tsp. cinnamon
½ tsp. salt
½ tsp. allspice
1 ½ cups canned pumpkin (from a 16-oz. can)
1 (14 ½-oz.) can evaporated milk or 1 ½ cups light cream
½ cup heavy cream

Mix 1 (10-oz.) pkg. pie crust mix with ¼ cup ice water and roll out to fit a 9-inch pie plate. Finish edge of crust with a high, fluted rim and set aside.

Make filling by beating together 3 eggs, ½ cup sugar, ¼ cup dark molasses, 1 teaspoon each ginger and cinnamon and ½ teaspoon each salt and allspice. Add 1 ½ cups canned pumpkin and 1 (14½-oz.) can evaporated milk (or 1 ½ cups light cream). Beat thoroughly to blend.

Pour into prepared pie shell. Bake 15 minutes at 425°, then 40 minutes more at 350°, until a knife inserted in center of pie comes out clean.

Serve pie hot with ½ cup heavy cream; or serve cold with ½ cup heavy cream whipped and piped decoratively around edge of pie. Serves 6.

❋ *Note:* Tradition calls for a choice of Mincemeat and Pumpkin Pie to be given at Thanksgiving. Try a variation on this old theme by serving a *combination* Mincemeat-Pumpkin Pie. Spread 1 ½ cups prepared mincemeat over the bottom of an unbaked 9-inch pie crust. Top with pumpkin filling as above and bake as directed.

FRANKFURTER KRANZER

2 (17-oz.) pkgs. pound cake mix
4 eggs
1 cup water

FROSTING:
4 cups sifted confectioners sugar
½ cup softened butter or margarine
½ cup heavy cream
1 cup finely crushed peanut brittle
Angelica
Cinnamon hots

Grease and flour an 8-cup ring mold. Prepare 2 (17-oz.) pkgs. pound cake mix according to label directions, using 4 eggs and 1 cup water. Bake in prepared ring mold 1 to 1¼ hours at 325°, until a cake tester inserted in center comes out clean. Cool in pan 5 minutes. Remove from pan and cool completely on wire rack. Cut in half crosswise.

Make filling by blending 4 cups sifted confectioners sugar into ½ cup softened butter or margarine, alternating with ½ cup heavy cream. Beat until smooth. Fold in 1 cup finely crushed peanut brittle.

Place bottom section of pound cake on serving plate. Spread with ½ cup frosting. Set top section in place and swirl top and sides of cake with remaining frosting. Decorate edge of cake with a wreath of holly leaves and berries made from angelica and cinnamon hots, or use real holly. Serves 12.

❋ *Note:* Angelica is candied rhubarb from France. Substitute green candied citron if you can't find it.

Alternately, bake the cake in a 10-inch bundt pan which gives the sides a most decorative effect. Split the cake into 4 layers. Divide frosting in three parts to sandwich layers together. Sprinkle with sifted confectioners sugar before serving. Decorate as directed.

BAGELS

1 pkg. dry active yeast
½ cup warm water
¼ cup salad oil
1 egg
3 cups sifted all-purpose flour
2 Tb. sugar
1 ½ tsp. salt
4 qts. boiling water
2 egg yolks
2 Tb. water

In a large mixing bowl, dissolve 1 pkg. dry active yeast in ½ cup warm water. Beat in ¼ cup salad oil and 1 egg.
Sift together 3 cups sifted all-purpose flour, 2 tablespoons sugar and 1 ½ teaspoons salt. Stir vigorously into yeast and water. Knead mixture on a floured board. Return to bowl and cover. Let rise in a warm place until doubled in volume.
Turn onto floured board. Knead at least 5 minutes (preferably 10 minutes). Divide dough into 12 even pieces. Roll each piece on floured board to a 9-inch strip. Dampen and pinch ends together. Place 6 of the bagels on a floured cookie sheet and set in preheated broiler 6 inches from source of heat. Broil 1-2 minutes, or until golden.
Drop bagels, uncooked side down, into 4 qts. rapidly boiling water in a large kettle. Cook, uncovered, over medium heat 10 to 15 minutes. Remove with a slotted spoon and place uncooked side up on cookie sheet. Bake 10 minutes at 400°. Brush with a little egg glaze made by beating together 2 egg yolks and 2 tablespoons water. Return bagels to oven and bake 5 minutes more, or until they are crispy and golden brown. Repeat process with 6 remaining bagels. Makes 12.

❊ Note: After brushing the bagels with egg glaze, bagels may be sprinkled with poppy seeds, coarse salt or onion flakes. Though this recipe takes some time, we feel the results are special enough to warrant the trouble.

CHALLAH

2 pkgs. dry active yeast
2 cups warm water
¼ cup vegetable shortening
8 cups sifted all-purpose flour
3 eggs, beaten
1 Tb. salt
1 Tb. sugar
2 egg yolks
2 Tb. water

In a large mixing bowl, dissolve 2 pkgs. dry active yeast in 2 cups warm water. Add ¼ cup vegetable shortening and stir to dissolve. Blend in 1 cup sifted all-purpose flour (reserve remaining 7 cups). Cover bowl and allow to rise 30 minutes.

Beat in remaining 7 cups flour, gradually adding 3 eggs, beaten. Stir in 1 tablespoon each salt and sugar. Turn out onto a well-floured board and knead until dough is smooth and elastic. Return to clean and lightly greased mixing bowl. Cover dough with damp cloth and let rise until doubled in volume.

Knead again on a floured board 5 minutes. Slice off one-third of dough and cut remaining dough in 3 even strips. Twist strips into a braid. Dampen all ends and tuck under to form an even shape. Place on a greased baking sheet and brush top with a little water. Divide remaining dough in 3 parts and braid; then place down center of large braid. Cover and let rise again, until doubled in bulk.

Brush challah well with egg glaze made by beating together 2 egg yolks and 2 tablespoons water. Bake 1 to 1¼ hours at 375°, until dark brown, crusty and hollow-sounding when tapped. Makes 1 large challah.

❋ *Note:* In expert Jewish kitchens, the water left over from boiling potatoes is used to dissolve yeast. If you have any, warm it and use it instead of the water. Also, a pinch of saffron may be crumbled into water to give the traditional flavor and yellow color.

THREE KINGS' LOAF

1 (13 ¾ -oz.) pkg. hot roll mix
¾ cup warm water
1 egg
½ tsp. cinnamon
½ tsp. allspice

FILLING:
¼ cup butter or margarine
2 Tb. light brown sugar
2 cups toasted coconut, crushed
1 cup chopped, blanched almonds
½ tsp. almond extract
1 egg white, slightly beaten

Prepare according to label directions 1 (13¾-oz.) pkg. hot roll mix, using ¾ cup water and 1 egg, adding ½ teaspoon each cinnamon and allspice. Cover bowl with damp cloth and set in a warm place. Allow to rise 30 minutes, or until doubled in bulk. *To prepare filling:* Cream together ¼ cup butter or margarine and 2 tablespoons light brown sugar. Stir in 2 cups toasted coconut, crushed, 1 cup chopped, blanched almonds and ½ teaspoon almond extract.

To assemble, roll out dough into a 9-inch square. Brush with a little of 1 egg white, slightly beaten. Spread filling over dough to within 1 inch of edge, and roll up, jelly roll fashion. Pinch both ends and seam to seal well. Place, seam side down, in a well-greased 9x5x3-inch loaf pan. Cover with damp cloth and let dough rise again until it rounds over top of pan.

Brush with remaining egg white and bake 40 to 45 minutes at 375°. Cool in pan on wire rack 5 minutes. Remove loaf from pan to rack and cool completely. Serves 10 to 12.

HONEY CAKE (LEKACH)

4 eggs
1 cup sugar
½ cup honey
½ cup hot black coffee
¼ cup salad oil
¾ cup golden raisins
¾ cup coarsely chopped walnuts
½ cup finely chopped, candied citron
3 ½ cups sifted all-purpose flour
2 tsp. baking powder
1 tsp. salt
1 tsp. grated lemon rind
½ tsp. allspice
½ tsp. cinnamon
¼ tsp. powdered cloves
2 Tb. brandy

Beat 4 eggs at high speed until light and creamy. Gradually add 1 cup sugar, beating until mixture is thick and lemon-colored. Blend ½ cup honey with ½ cup hot black coffee and ¼ cup salad oil. Cool and fold into beaten eggs. Fold in ¾ cup each golden raisins and coarsely chopped walnuts and ½ cup finely chopped, candied citron.

Sift together 3½ cups sifted all-purpose flour, 2 teaspoons baking powder, 1 teaspoon each salt and grated lemon rind, ½ teaspoon each allspice and cinnamon and ¼ teaspoon powdered cloves. Fold into mixture, with 2 tablespoons brandy.

Pour into a greased and floured 15½x10½x1½-inch jelly roll pan that has been lined with waxed paper. Bake 45 to 60 minutes at 350°, or until browned, and surface springs back when lightly touched. Invert cake onto wire rack and peel off paper. Turn right side up onto second rack. Cool completely on rack before cutting into squares and diamond shapes. Serves 12.

COLONIAL VIRGINIA CAKE

1 cup softened butter or margarine
1 cup sugar
4 eggs
¼ cup Madeira or sweet sherry
2 cups sifted all-purpose flour
1 tsp. baking powder
1 tsp. grated orange rind
Dry, unseasoned bread crumbs

FROSTING:
1 cup sifted confectioners sugar
1 Tb. softened butter or margarine
1 Tb. Madeira or sweet sherry
1 tsp. grated orange rind
6 candied cherry halves
Candied citron leaves

Beat 1 cup softened butter or margarine with 1 cup sugar until light and fluffy. Beat in 4 eggs, 1 at a time, beating well after each addition. Beat in ¼ cup Madeira (or sweet sherry). Sift together 2 cups sifted all-purpose flour and 1 teaspoon baking powder. Fold flour gently into egg mixture, adding 1 teaspoon grated orange rind.

Grease a 5-cup fluted mold (or a 9x5x3-inch loaf pan). Sprinkle evenly with dry, unseasoned bread crumbs. Pour cake batter into pan and bake 1 hour at 350°, until cake tester comes out clean when inserted in center. Cool in pan on wire rack 5 minutes; then remove from pan to rack and cool completely.

To make frosting: Blend 1 cup sifted confectioners sugar, 1 tablespoon each butter or margarine and Madeira (or sweet sherry) and 1 teaspoon grated orange rind. Swirl frosting over top of cake and decorate with 6 candied cherry halves and candied citron leaves arranged like a wreath in center. Serves 12.

MARTHA WASHINGTON'S GREAT CAKE

1 cup butter or margarine
1 cup sugar
6 eggs
3 cups, sifted all-purpose flour
2 tsp. baking powder
½ tsp. mace
½ tsp. salt
½ tsp. nutmeg
1 cup diced citron
1 cup diced crystallized ginger
1 cup coarsely chopped almonds
½ cup flaked almonds

FROSTING:
1 cup confectioners sugar
1-2 Tb. brandy

Cream together 1 cup each butter or margarine and sugar. Beat in 6 eggs, 1 at a time. Fold in 3 cups sifted all-purpose flour which has been re-sifted with 2 teaspoons baking powder, and ½ teaspoon each mace, salt and nutmeg.

Stir in 1 cup each diced citron, crystallized ginger and coarsely chopped almonds. Grease a 9-inch bundt pan very well (or use an angel food pan) and press over sides and base ½ cup flaked almonds to line pan. Spoon in batter. Bake 1-1¼ hours at 325°, or until a cake tester comes out clean when inserted in center. Cool cake in pan on wire rack 5 minutes. Remove from pan to rack and cool completely.

To make frosting: Blend 1 cup confectioners sugar with 1-2 tablespoons brandy. Spoon over cake so frosting runs over top and drizzles down sides. Serves 12 generously.

PRINCE PHILLIP CAKE

1 (18 ½ -oz.) pkg. fudge-marble cake mix
1 ⅓ cups water
2 eggs
¾ cup apricot preserves
¼ cup maple blended syrup
2 (8-oz.) cans almond paste

Blend 1 (18½-oz.) pkg. fudge-marble cake mix (reserving packet of chocolate), 1⅓ cups water and 2 eggs. Beat 2 minutes at medium speed. Grease and flour 2 (8x8x2-inch) pans and pour 3 cups batter into one of the pans.

Mix packet of chocolate into remaining batter. Pour into second prepared pan. Bake both cakes 30 to 35 minutes at 350°. Remove from pans and cool. Level cakes, if necessary, and trim off crusty edges. Cut each cake lengthwise into 4 strips. Heat ¾ cup apricot preserves with ¼ cup maple blended syrup. Use to brush all cut surfaces of chocolate and vanilla cake strips. Press 2 strips chocolate and 2 strips vanilla cake together in a checkerboard arrangement. Wrap tightly in plastic wrap or foil. Repeat, using remaining 2 cake strips. Refrigerate both cakes at least 30 minutes.

To assemble, roll out 1 of the (8-oz.) cans almond paste on a lightly floured board to measure 13x8 inches. Trim edges. Brush with a little remaining apricot-maple mixture. Unwrap one cake and set in center of almond paste strip. Wrap cake completely in almond paste. Press joining seam and turn cake over so that the seam side is down. Flute the 2 long edges with fingers. Decorate with almond paste trimmings formed into flowers. Repeat, using second can of almond paste and remaining checkerboard cake. Makes 2 cakes, each serving 6 to 8.

HOLIDAY COFFEE CAKE

1 pkg. dry active yeast
1 1/3 cups warm water
1 (19-oz.) pkg. white cake mix
2 eggs

TOPPING:
1 (8-oz.) pkg. pitted prunes
1 (8-oz.) pkg. pitted apricots
1/2 cup water
1/2 cup sugar
1/2 tsp. almond extract

STREUSEL:
1 1/2 cups sifted all-purpose flour
1/2 cup butter or margarine
1/2 cup sugar
1 tsp. cinnamon

Dissolve 1 pkg. dry active yeast in 1 1/3 cups warm water. Prepare 1 (19-oz.) pkg. white cake mix according to label directions, adding 2 eggs and the water in which yeast was dissolved. Pour batter into a well-greased angel food cake pan. Cover with damp cloth and let rise in a warm place at least 30 minutes.

To prepare topping: Cook 1 (8-oz.) pkg. each pitted prunes and pitted apricots 15 minutes in 1/2 cup each water and sugar and 1/2 teaspoon almond extract. Chop fruit (water will be absorbed) and cool. Set aside.

To prepare streusel: With a fork or pastry cutter, blend together 1 1/2 cups sifted all-purpose flour and 1/2 cup butter or margarine until mixture resembles coarse cornmeal. Stir in 1/2 cup sugar and 1 teaspoon cinnamon. Set aside.

Bake cake 45 minutes at 350°. Remove from oven and spread fruit topping evenly over surface; then sprinkle with prepared streusel. Bake 15 to 20 minutes more. Cool in pan on wire rack 5 minutes; remove cake from pan and cool on rack 15 minutes more. Cake may be served slightly warm or completely cooled. Serves 15 to 20 generously.

BÛCHE DE NOËL

4 eggs
¾ cup sugar
¾ cup sifted all-purpose flour
¾ tsp. baking powder
¼ tsp. salt
1 tsp. vanilla extract
2 (2 ¾ -oz.) pkgs. almond macaroons, crumbled (about 2 cups)
1 ½ cups fresh bread crumbs
1 cup chopped almonds
½ cup red currant jelly
¼ cup marsala or white rum

FROSTING:
1 ½ cups heavy cream or 2 (2 ⅛ -oz.) pkgs. whipped topping mix
¼ cup instant powdered chocolate drink
¼ cup sifted unsweetened cocoa

Grease a 15½x10½x1-inch jelly roll pan and line with waxed paper. Grease paper and set aside.

In a large bowl, beat 4 eggs until foamy. Gradually add ¾ cup sugar and continue beating 5 minutes more. Sift together ¾ cup sifted all-purpose flour, ¾ teaspoon baking powder and ¼ teaspoon salt. Add to egg mixture, blending at low speed until well mixed. Stir in 1 teaspoon vanilla extract and pour batter into jelly roll pan.

Bake 15 to 18 minutes at 350°, or until surface springs back when lightly touched. Invert onto a sugared towel and peel off waxed paper. Trim away a ½-inch strip all around. Roll up cake and towel and let cool 30 minutes on wire rack.

Make filling by blending 2 (2¾-oz.) pkgs. almond macaroons, crumbled, 1 ½ cups fresh bread crumbs, 1 cup chopped almonds, ½ cup red currant jelly and ¼ cup marsala (or white rum). Unroll cake and remove towel. Press roll gently to flatten and spread with prepared filling. Re-roll, using towel to reshape roll if necessary. Place seam side down on serving plate and chill.

To make frosting: Beat 1 ½ cups heavy cream until stiff and fold in ¼ cup each instant powdered chocolate drink and sifted unsweetened cocoa (or prepare 2 [2⅛-oz.] pkgs. whipped topping mix according to label directions, and fold in chocolate drink and cocoa).

142

To assemble, slice both ends diagonally from chilled roll to a depth of 1 inch. Place one end on top of roll to resemble the beginning of a branch. Set in place with a little frosting. Frost Bûche de Noël all over. Draw tines of fork across frosting to give a bark-like effect. Decorate with holly, if desired. Serve chilled. Serves 6 to 8.

❋ *Note:* This is supposed to resemble the Yule Log, and is a favorite treat in France during the Christmas season.

GREEK NEW YEAR'S BREAD

2 (13 ¾ -oz.) pkgs. hot roll mix
1 ¼ cups warm milk
2 eggs
¼ cup honey
½ tsp. cinnamon
½ tsp. nutmeg
1 cup chopped almonds
2 Tb. honey
2 Tb. flaked almonds

Prepare 2 (13¾-oz.) pkgs. hot roll mix, using 1 ¼ cups warm milk in which 2 pkgs. active dry yeast from mix have been dissolved. Beat in 2 eggs and ¼ cup honey. Stir in flour from hot roll mix, together with ½ teaspoon each cinnamon and nutmeg. Stir very well. Set to rise, covered, 30 minutes in a warm place.
Turn dough onto a floured board and knead well. Knead in 1 cup chopped almonds. Place in a round, 1-1 ½-qt. oven-proof casserole and allow to rise again, until doubled in volume. Bake 40-50 minutes at 375°, or until golden brown and sounds hollow when rapped. Loosen from casserole and cool on wire rack.
While still warm, brush cake with 2 tablespoons honey and sprinkle with 2 tablespoons flaked almonds. Cool completely. Serves 10 to 12 generously.

CHAPTER EIGHT / LIGHT HOLIDAY DESSERTS

Rich *and* light—holiday dessert spectaculars that everyone dreams of. Our approach to the question of a grand finale to a grand meal is that *grand* needn't equal *heavy*. Riz Royale, for instance, is a creamy rice pudding mold with candied fruit folded in. Baked Alaska, basically ice cream in a meringue shell, is ravishing . . . and *light*. Crème Amandine is custard with almonds, festive and welcome after a heavy meal. Mousses, parfaits, soufflés—this is their hour, when what's come before in the way of a main course dictates that what comes last should be full of sweetness and light. Calorie counters, forewarned being forearmed, proceed at their peril . . .

BAKED ALASKA

3 pts. rum raisin or maple walnut ice cream
1 baked, 9-inch cake layer (at least 1-inch thick)
¼ cup white rum or orange juice
1 cup egg whites (6 to 8 eggs)
¼ tsp. cream of tartar
¼ tsp. salt
¾ cup superfine sugar

Line a 6-cup bowl by criss-crossing 6 (3-inch) strips aluminum foil. Foil should extend 1 inch beyond edge of bowl. Firmly pack lined bowl with 3 pts. rum raisin (or maple walnut) ice cream which has been standing in refrigerator 30 minutes to soften. Set in freezer at least 1 hour, until ice cream is firm.

Place a double thickness of heavy duty foil on a baking sheet. Place 1 baked, 9-inch cake layer on foil and sprinkle with ¼ cup white rum or orange juice. In large bowl of electric mixer, beat 1 cup egg whites with ¼ teaspoon each cream of tartar and salt until egg whites are stiff. Gradually beat in ¾ cup superfine sugar and continue beating until stiff peaks are formed.

Unmold ice cream onto cake layer, removing foil strips. Swirl meringue completely over cake and ice cream. Place immediately on lowest rack in oven and bake 3 to 5 minutes at 475°, or until meringue is pale golden. Trim away excess foil and serve at once. Serves 12.

❋ *Note:* Regular granulated sugar may also be used in this recipe, instead of the superfine; just make sure it is thoroughly dissolved in the meringue (it may take a bit more beating than with superfine).

MAPLE RIZ ROYALE

1 envelope unflavored gelatine
2 Tb. cold water
1 (3-oz.) pkg. egg custard mix
2 cups heavy cream or 2 (2 ⅛ -oz.) pkgs. whipped topping mix
1 cup mixed candied fruit
½ cup chopped pistachios
½ cup maple blended syrup
3 cups cooked rice
Pecans

Soften 1 envelope unflavored gelatine in 2 tablespoons cold water and set aside. Prepare 1 (3-oz.) pkg. egg custard mix according to directions and remove from heat. Stir in softened gelatine to dissolve. Press plastic wrap or waxed paper on surface of custard and chill until syrupy. Next, whip 1 cup of the heavy cream until stiff (or prepare 1 of the [2⅛-oz.] pkgs. whipped topping mix according to directions).

Add 1 cup mixed candied fruit, ½ cup each chopped pistachios and maple blended syrup and 3 cups cooked rice to syrupy custard mixture. Mix well, then fold in whipped cream or whipped topping mix. Pour into a lightly-oiled 6-cup mold and chill until thoroughly set—at least 3 hours.

To serve, dip mold into hot water no more than 20 seconds and invert custard onto chilled serving platter. Return to refrigerator. Whip remaining 1 cup heavy cream (or prepare remaining 1 [2⅛-oz.] pkg. whipped topping mix). Place 3 puffs whipped cream on top of mold and pipe remaining whipped cream in rosettes around base. Tuck a pecan half between each rosette. Serves 10 to 12. *(See photograph.)*

BABA AU RHUM WITH MAPLE

1 (13 ¾ -oz.) pkg. hot roll mix
¾ cup lukewarm water
½ cup sugar
3 egg yolks, lightly beaten
¼ cup melted butter or margarine, cooled
1 cup apricot jam
1 cup maple blended syrup
½ cup rum

In a medium bowl, mix envelope of yeast from 1 (13¾-oz.) pkg. hot roll mix with ¾ cup lukewarm water. Stir until dissolved. Add ½ cup sugar and 3 egg yolks, lightly beaten. Add remaining ingredients in hot roll mix and blend thoroughly. Cover bowl with damp cloth and allow dough to rise until doubled in bulk —about 1 hour.

Beat in ¼ cup melted butter or margarine, cooled, 1 tablespoon at a time. Place dough in a well-greased, 9-inch angel food cake pan, cover and allow to rise again until doubled in bulk—about 45 minutes to 1 hour.

Bake 25 minutes at 375°, or until Baba is golden brown. Immediately turn onto serving plate and let stand 15 minutes. Spread all over with 1 cup apricot jam which has been rubbed through a sieve or whirred in blender 60 seconds.

Combine 1 cup maple blended syrup and ½ cup rum, mixing well. Spoon over apricot-glazed cake, a few spoonfuls at a time, until maple-rum sauce is soaked into cake and cake is cooled. Serves 8 to 10.

❈ *Note:* This marvelous, no-knead cake can be made even more dazzling. Heat an extra ¼ cup rum, ignite and pour over cake. Bring cake to table in a blaze of glory!

OEUFS À LA NEIGE

4 egg whites
¼ tsp. cream of tartar
¼ tsp. salt
½ cup superfine sugar
3 cups milk
1 (4½-oz.) pkg. egg custard mix
1 egg yolk
1 tsp. almond extract
1 cup dark corn syrup

Beat 4 egg whites with ¼ tsp. each cream of tartar and salt until very stiff. Gradually beat in ½ cup superfine sugar until egg whites are stiff and shiny. In a large skillet, heat 3 cups milk just to a simmer. Drop meringue by the tablespoon into simmering milk and cook 2 to 3 minutes. Turn each meringue gently and cook 2 to 3 minutes more. With a slotted spoon, remove meringues and set on a towel to drain thoroughly. When drained, carefully transfer to a lightly-buttered plate.

Measure remaining milk in skillet, adding more if necessary to measure 3 cups. Prepare 1 (4½-oz.) pkg. egg custard mix according to directions, using the 3 cups milk in skillet and 1 egg yolk. Stir in 1 teaspoon almond extract and pour into serving bowl. Place a piece of plastic wrap or waxed paper onto surface of custard, cool slightly, then chill.

Just before serving, boil 1 cup dark corn syrup to 230° on candy thermometer (soft thread stage). Arrange poached meringues on custard in serving bowl and spoon boiled syrup over meringues. Serve at once. Serves 6.

PARIS BREST

1 recipe Cream Puff Pastry (see following recipe)
2 cups heavy cream or 3 (2 ⅛-oz.) pkgs. whipped topping mix
¼ cup confectioners sugar
1 tsp. almond extract
2 Tb. light corn syrup
2 Tb. chopped, toasted walnuts

Cut a 9-inch circle of heavy brown paper or heavy duty foil and set in center of a cookie sheet. Oil circle lightly. Prepare 1 recipe Cream Puff Pastry (see following recipe) and spoon heaping tablespoons of pastry around paper circle, making a complete ring and leaving a 4-inch circle free in center. Smooth pastry with spatula and bake 50 to 60 minutes at 400°, or until brown.

Remove pastry from oven, turn off oven and slice top from baked ring with a sharp knife. Remove any soft dough from inside. Place top of ring upside down on cookie sheet next to bottom of ring. Return to oven, leaving oven door open, 15 minutes. Remove and set both pieces of pastry on wire rack to cool (away from draughts).

Whip 2 cups heavy cream with ¼ cup confectioners sugar and 1 teaspoon almond extract (or prepare 3 [2⅛-oz.] pkgs. whipped topping mix according to directions and add 1 teaspoon almond extract). Set bottom of pastry ring on serving dish and fill with whipped cream. Place top lightly on whipped cream and brush with 2 tablespoons light corn syrup. Sprinkle 2 tablespoons chopped, toasted almonds over top. Serves 6 to 8.

❋ Note: Other flavoring ideas—substitute orange extract for almond extract and top filled pastry ring with 2 tablespoons coarsely grated orange rind instead of almonds. Or, beat ½ cup powdered cocoa mix and 1 teaspoon powdered instant coffee into the 2 cups heavy cream and top ring with 2 tablespoons coarsely grated semi-sweet chocolate.

ICE CREAM PUFFS WITH CHOCOLATE GLAZE

1 cup water
½ cup butter or margarine
1 cup sifted flour
4 large eggs
1 ½ qts. coffee ice cream
2 cups confectioners sugar
½ cup chocolate syrup

Bring 1 cup water and ½ cup butter or margarine to a boil. Add 1 cup sifted flour all at once and beat until mixture leaves the sides of the saucepan. Remove from heat and beat in 4 large eggs, 1 at a time. Beat very well after adding each egg, continuing to beat until dough is shiny. Drop dough by tablespoons on to an ungreased cookie sheet 2 inches apart to make 12 puffs. Bake 45 to 50 minutes at 400°, or until golden brown. Cool puffs on wire rack (away from draughts).
Split cooled cream puffs in half, removing any soft dough from center. Fill each with ½ cup coffee ice cream (from 1 ½ qts.). Combine 2 cups confectioners sugar and ½ cup chocolate syrup and spoon a little of this glaze over each prepared cream puff. Serve at once. Makes 12.

❋ *Note:* If you're in a rush, buy cream puff shells at your local bakery . . . but think of the delight of making your own!
Butterscotch, fudge or nesselrode ice cream topping are excellent alternates for glazing these puffs. For a change, heat the toppings and pour over this dessert just before serving.

MAPLE MOUSSE

4 eggs, separated
1 cup maple blended syrup
1 cup heavy cream
¼ cup brandy
½ cup chopped walnuts

In upper portion of a double boiler, beat 4 egg yolks very well. Stir in 1 cup maple blended syrup. Cook, beating constantly with wire whisk or rotary beater over hot *(not boiling)* water until mixture thickens. Remove from heat.
Beat 4 egg whites until stiff. Gently fold hot maple syrup mixture into whites. Cool, then chill. Whip 1 cup heavy cream and fold into chilled pudding with ¼ cup brandy. Pour into 3 empty ice cube trays and place in freezer. Freeze at least 4-5 hours, stirring mousse once after the first hour of freezing time.
Spoon into individual serving dishes and sprinkle each serving with some of ½ cup chopped walnuts. Serves 6.

COEUR À LA CRÈME

1 (8-oz.) pkg. cream cheese, softened
1 cup small-curd cottage cheese, well drained
½ cup sour cream
½ cup heavy cream
2 Tb. confectioners sugar
½ tsp. vanilla extract
Fresh whole strawberries or strawberry preserves

Beat 1 (8-oz.) pkg. cream cheese, softened, until smooth. Stir in 1 cup small-curd cottage cheese, well drained, and ½ cup sour cream, mixing well. Whip ½ cup heavy cream with 2 tablespoons confectioners sugar and ½ teaspoon vanilla extract and fold into cheese mixture. Line a 2-cup heart-shaped mold or basket with a piece of damp cheesecloth. Spoon cheese mixture into mold and fold edges of cheesecloth over top. Refrigerate at least 8 hours, preferably overnight.
Unmold, remove cheesecloth and serve with fresh whole strawberries (or spread lightly with strawberry preserves). Serves 6.

CHESTNUT SOUFFLÉ

¼ cup butter or margarine
½ cup flour
¾ cup milk
½ cup sugar
6 eggs, separated
¼ cup brandy
1 cup canned chestnut puree (a 15½-oz. can)
½ tsp. cream of tartar
½ tsp. salt
Sugar

In a medium saucepan, melt ¼ cup butter or margarine. While off heat, stir in ½ cup flour, mixing until smooth. Gradually stir in ¾ cup milk and ½ cup sugar and return to heat. Bring to a boil, stirring constantly. Mixture will form a very thick batter which will pull away from sides of saucepan.

Remove from heat. Add 6 egg yolks, 1 at a time, beating vigorously after each. Beat in ¼ cup brandy and let cool 10 minutes, stirring once or twice. Stir in 1 cup canned chestnut puree.

In a large bowl, beat 6 egg whites with ½ teaspoon each cream of tartar and salt until whites are stiff but not dry. Fold into cooled chestnut mixture and turn gently into a 2-qt. soufflé dish that has been well-greased and heavily sprinkled with additional sugar. Bake 45 to 50 minutes at 375°, or until a cake tester inserted into side toward center comes out clean. Serve at once. Serves 6 to 8.

❊ Note: An ideal sauce for this soufflé is 1 cup heavy cream, stiffly beaten, gently combined with 2-4 tablespoons liqueur.

BAKLAVA

2 cups honey
2 (10-oz.) pkgs. frozen puff pastry shells, defrosted
3 cups finely chopped walnuts
1 cup heavy cream, whipped, or 1 (2 ⅛ -oz.) pkg.
   whipped topping mix

Boil 2 cups honey gently until reduced to 1 cup. Line an 8x8x2-inch pan with aluminum foil. Press 3 defrosted puff shells (from 2 [10-oz.] pkgs.) together and roll out on a floured surface to an 8½-inch square.

Place in bottom of foil-lined pan and sprinkle with 1 cup of the finely chopped walnuts. Drizzle ¼ cup reduced warm honey over nuts. Repeat layering process twice and top with a fourth square of plain pastry.

Score top of pastry in a diamond pattern with sharp knife. Bake 25 to 30 minutes at 425°, until pastry is brown. Cool in pan 10 minutes, then remove from pan and pull away foil. Brush surface with remaining ¼ cup warm honey. Serve with 1 cup heavy cream, whipped, or 1 (2⅛-oz.) pkg. whipped topping mix, prepared according to directions. Serves 8 to 10.

❊ *Note:* This is a very rich dessert and should only be served in tiny morsels. Unsweetened whipped cream or vanilla ice cream are essential to mellow the sweetness level. Baklava can be served as a cookie to accompany parfaits but must be tossed in finely chopped nuts to cover the honey so it can be picked up without sticky fingers.

Café
Brulot

Icy
Lemons

Maple
Riz
Royale

Hot
Posset

Champagne
Punch

Cranberry
Nog

LEMON-RASPBERRY PARFAIT

1 (3 ½ -oz.) pkg. lemon-flavored pudding and pie filling mix
½ cup sugar
2 ¼ cups water
2 eggs, separated
1 cup heavy cream, whipped
1 (10-oz.) pkg. frozen raspberries, thawed

In a saucepan, combine 1 (3½-oz.) pkg. lemon-flavored pudding and pie filling mix with ¼ cup each of the sugar and water. Add 2 egg yolks and blend well. Slowly stir in remaining 2 cups water and cook, stirring constantly, until mixture comes to a boil. Remove from heat.

Beat 2 egg whites until foamy. Gradually beat in remaining ¼ cup sugar until a stiff meringue is formed. Fold into hot pudding. Cool, then chill. Whip 1 cup heavy cream; set aside ½ cup whipped cream and fold rest into chilled pudding.

Whir 1 (10-oz.) pkg. frozen raspberries, thawed, in blender 30 seconds. Strain. Place alternate layers of lemon pudding and raspberry puree in parfait glasses and top each serving with some of the reserved ½ cup whipped cream. Serves 6 to 8.

ICY LEMONS

6 large lemons
1 qt. lemon sherbet
½ cup heavy cream
2 Tb. confectioners sugar
½ tsp. vanilla extract
Chocolate curls

Wash 6 large lemons and dry well. With a very sharp knife, cut off ⅓ of each lemon lengthwise. Scoop out pulp and discard. Scoop some of 1 qt. lemon sherbet into each lemon shell. Place in freezer.

Just before serving, whip ½ cup heavy cream with 2 tablespoons confectioners sugar and ½ teaspoon vanilla extract. Press through pastry tube (or metal pastry syringe) to form a rosette on top of each lemon. Decorate with chocolate curls made by gently pulling a vegetable scraper across side of 1-oz. squares semi-sweet chocolate. Serves 6. *(See photograph.)*

❋ *Note:* Whipped topping mix, prepared according to directions, may be used instead of the heavy cream, omitting sugar and vanilla extract called for above. And, of course, oranges and orange sherbet would do equally well for this recipe. (You'll need 1 qt. orange sherbet.)

FLAMING ANGEL CAKE

1 (15-oz.) pkg. angel food cake mix
1 cup apricot preserves
½ cup rum

Prepare 1 (15-oz.) pkg. angel food cake mix according to directions, bake and cool. Turn cooled cake onto serving plate. Combine 1 cup apricot preserves and ¼ cup of the rum in a small saucepan. Heat gently, stirring constantly to blend well. Spoon sauce over cake. Heat remaining ¼ cup rum, ignite and pour, flaming, over cake. Serves 6 to 8.

QUEEN OF PUDDINGS

6 slices white bread
½ cup golden raisins
4 eggs
¾ cup sugar
4 cups milk
1 tsp. vanilla extract
¼ tsp. nutmeg
1 cup seedless raspberry preserves or jelly
2 egg whites
2 Tb. sugar

Remove crusts from 6 slices white bread and cut each slice in half. Arrange in layers in a greased 1 ½-qt. baking dish, sprinkling each layer with some of ½ cup golden raisins (do not sprinkle any raisins on top layer).

Combine 4 eggs, ¾ cup sugar, 4 cups milk, 1 teaspoon vanilla extract and ¼ teaspoon nutmeg. Beat well and heat gently just to dissolve sugar. Pour mixture over bread and place baking dish in a pan containing 1 inch hot water. Bake 50 to 60 minutes at 350°, or until a knife inserted in center comes out clean. Remove dish from water and cool.

Spread top of cooled custard with 1 cup seedless raspberry preserves (or jelly). Beat 2 egg whites until foamy. Gradually beat in 2 tablespoons sugar and continue beating until a thick, glossy meringue is formed. Spoon meringue around edge and serve (do not bake). Serves 6 to 8. *(See photograph.)*

✳ *Note:* Thinly sliced apples or thinly sliced canned, drained, peaches, pears or apricots can be substituted for raisins, to make a lighter dessert. The meringue can be browned quickly at 450° for 3 to 4 minutes if desired.

CRANBERRIES IN SNOW

1 (19-oz.) pkg. yellow cake mix
1 cup fresh cranberries
1 cup sugar
½ cup water
6 egg whites
¼ tsp. cream of tartar
¾ cup sugar

Prepare 1 (19-oz.) pkg. yellow cake mix according to directions and bake in 24 medium cupcake tins 15 to 20 minutes at 350°. Cool. Combine 1 cup each fresh cranberries and sugar and ½ cup water in a saucepan and bring to a boil. Cook over medium heat 5 to 8 minutes, then cool.

Beat 6 egg whites with ¼ teaspoon cream of tartar until foamy. Add ¾ cup sugar gradually, beating constantly until meringue is glossy and forms stiff peaks.

Place 12 of the cupcakes onto a cookie sheet and frost each with meringue (save the other 12 cupcakes for another day). Bake meringue-frosted cupcakes 5 minutes at 450°, or until meringue is very lightly browned. Cool and top each with some of the cooked, cooled cranberries. Serves 12. *(See photograph.)*

❋ *Note:* In the interests of saving time, you could buy unfrosted cupcakes from your bakery and use canned whole cranberry sauce instead of preparing the sauce from scratch. *Almost* the same.

Any small berry fruit may be substituted for cranberries. Frozen raspberries would be ideal. Drain, and make sauce from liquid by blending with 1 cup red wine and thickening with 2 tablespoons cornstarch.

FRUIT MELBA

1 (10-oz.) pkg. frozen raspberries
2 Tb. fresh lime juice
¼ cup sweet sherry
4 cups assorted canned fruits, drained
1 pt. vanilla ice cream

Place 1 (10-oz.) pkg. frozen raspberries and 2 tablespoons fresh lime juice in blender container and whir 30 seconds. Strain and stir in ¼ cup sweet sherry. Set aside.

To serve, divide 4 cups assorted canned fruits, drained, between 6 serving dishes. Top each with a scoop of vanilla ice cream (from 1 pt.). Spoon fruit sauce over top and serve. Serves 6.

✳ *Note:* Lemon juice may be substituted for the lime juice called for above, and frozen, defrosted fruits, drained, may be used instead of the canned fruits.

MINCEMEAT PEAR PIE

1 (10-oz.) pkg. pie crust mix
2 lbs. firm-ripe pears
1 (17-oz.) jar mincemeat with brandy and rum
2 Tb. heavy cream

Prepare 1 (10-oz.) pkg. pie crust mix according to directions. On a lightly floured surface roll out ⅔ of dough to ⅛-inch thickness. Fit into 9-inch pie plate. Trim pastry edges. Wrap remaining dough in plastic wrap or waxed paper. Set aside. Cut 2 lbs. firm-ripe pears into quarters, pare and remove cores. Cut each quarter into 3 slices and arrange over bottom of pastry-lined plate. Top pears with 1 (17-oz.) jar mincemeat with brandy and rum. Moisten rim of crust with water. Roll out remaining dough and place on top of pie. Trim crust to hang over no more than ¼ inch. Turn edge under and flute. Cut 2 or 3 slits in top crust to allow steam to escape. Brush pastry with 2 tablespoons heavy cream and bake 30 to 35 minutes at 425°, until crust is deep golden brown. Serve hot or cold. Serves 6 to 8.

CRÈME AMANDINE

2 envelopes unflavored gelatine
6 cups light cream
2 (4½-oz.) pkgs. egg custard mix
3 egg yolks
1 tsp. almond extract
1 cup heavy cream
¼ cup slivered, toasted almonds
¼ cup honey

Soak 2 envelopes unflavored gelatine in 1 cup of the light cream. In a large saucepan, combine 2 (4½-oz.) pkgs. egg custard mix with remaining 5 cups light cream and 3 egg yolks and cook according to label directions. Add gelatine-cream mixture to hot custard and stir until gelatine is dissolved. Stir in 1 teaspoon almond extract and pour custard into a lightly-oiled 2-qt. ring mold. Cool, then chill until set—at least 2 hours.
Unmold custard onto chilled serving plate and return to refrigerator. Whip 1 cup heavy cream and spoon into center of custard ring. Sprinkle whipped cream with ¼ cup slivered, toasted almonds and drizzle ¼ cup honey over all. Serves 6 to 8.

MACÉDOINE OF WINTER FRUITS

4 cups cut-up assorted fresh fruits
1 cup water
½ cup sugar
¼ cup Kirsch

Place 4 cups cut-up assorted fresh fruits in a large bowl. In a small saucepan combine 1 cup water and ½ cup sugar. Bring to a boil, reduce heat and simmer 5 minutes, stirring to dissolve sugar. Cool. Stir in ¼ cup Kirsch. Pour over fruits and let stand at room temperature at least 1 hour to blend flavors. Chill before serving. Serves 6.

❋ Note: Apples, pears, grapes, oranges, tangerines and bananas are winter fruits. Strawberries are a year-round fruit thanks to the Mexican-Southern California crop and airplanes.

MAPLE CHIFFON PIE

1 (3-oz.) pkg. orange-flavored gelatine
1 cup boiling water
¾ cup maple blended syrup
1 tsp. grated lemon rind
4 egg whites
1 (9-inch) pie shell, baked

Dissolve 1 (3-oz.) pkg. orange-flavored gelatine in 1 cup boiling water and stir to dissolve gelatine. Add ¾ cup maple blended syrup and 1 teaspoon grated lemon rind. Cool until mixture is the consistency of unbeaten egg white. Beat 4 egg whites until stiff. Beat gelatine mixture until light and fluffy and immediately fold beaten egg whites into gelatine. Turn gently into 1 (9-inch) pie shell, baked. Chill 1-2 hours. Serves 6 to 8.

ORANGE BAVARIAN (variation): Dissolve 1 (3-oz.) pkg. orange-flavored gelatine in 1 cup hot water. Add ½ cup cold water. Chill until syrupy. Rinse 5-cup mold with cold water. Pour gelatine to depth of ⅛ inch, to line bottom.
Fill jelly roll pan with crushed ice. Lay mold on side in crushed ice and spoon in syrupy gelatine, "spinning" mold around to coat sides evenly. Add more syrupy gelatine and spin mold to build up gelatine layer to ⅛ inch. Chill lined mold 20 minutes. Add maple chiffon filling. Chill at least 2 hours more. Dip in hot water to unmold. Serves 6 to 8. *(See photograph.)*

CHAPTER NINE / FESTIVE DRINKS

Here's to holiday cheer, and to the many wonderful ways of toasting the season! How? With nogs, mulled concoctions, punches and toddies (to name but a few). Some are alcoholic, others are not, but they're delightful brews, all, to warm the heart and gladden the soul: chilly or hot, spicy or sweet, fizzy or smooth, take your pick and raise your glass on high. Whether your pleasure is something warming after a winter afternoon's walk, or you're looking for something particularly right for a party, here you'll find just what's needed to fill any gathering with the proper festive spirit.

GINGER CLARET PUNCH

1 cup sugar
1 cup water
½ tsp. nutmeg
½ tsp. ginger
1 (2-inch) piece stick cinnamon
6 whole cloves
2 (1-inch) strips lemon peel
2 (1-inch) strips orange peel
3 cups claret or domestic Burgundy wine
2 cups ginger ale, chilled
Thin orange slices
Thin lemon slices

In a medium saucepan, combine 1 cup each sugar and water, ½ teaspoon each nutmeg and ginger, 1 (2-inch) piece stick cinnamon and 6 whole cloves stuck into 2 (1-inch) strips each lemon peel and orange peel. Bring to a boil, stirring to dissolve sugar. Reduce heat and simmer, uncovered, 5 minutes. Remove from heat, cover and let stand until cool.

With slotted spoon, remove cinnamon stick, clove-studded lemon peel and orange peel. Add 3 cups claret (or domestic Burgundy wine). Chill. To serve, add 2 cups ginger ale, chilled, and garnish with thin orange and lemon slices. Makes 6 cups.

✳ Note: To serve this as a hot punch, omit ginger ale and add wine to the hot, spiced sugar syrup. Bring again to a simmer and serve hot. Yield will be reduced to 4 cups.

SANTA'S NIGHTCAP

1 cup gin
1 cup light rum
¼ cup lime juice
¼ cup maple blended syrup

Combine 1 cup gin, 1 cup light rum and ¼ cup each lime juice and maple blended syrup. Stir well to mix; pour over crushed ice in cocktail glasses. Makes 2½ cups.

HOT EGGNOG

3 eggs, separated
4 cups (1 qt.) light cream
¾ cup sugar
1 cup light rum
2 tsp. vanilla extract
Nutmeg

In large bowl of electric mixer, beat 3 egg yolks at high speed until thick and lemon-colored. In a large saucepan, heat 4 cups light cream with ½ cup sugar, stirring until sugar dissolves and mixture is simmering. Gradually pour mixture over egg yolks, beating constantly. Stir in 1 cup light rum and 2 teaspoons vanilla extract, mixing well.

In small bowl of electric mixer, beat egg whites (with clean beaters) until frothy. Add remaining ¼ cup sugar gradually, beating constantly until a thick, glossy meringue is formed. Serve eggnog hot, topped with meringue and a light sprinkle of nutmeg. Makes about 5½ cups.

※ *Note:* To serve cold, cool egg yolk and cream mixture, then chill. Just prior to serving, stir in vanilla extract and rum. Top with meringue and sprinkle lightly with nutmeg. Eggnog may be prepared very tastily, hot or cold, without rum, in which case the yield would be about 4½ cups.

In a hurry? Use 1 qt. commercial eggnog: heat to a simmer, stirring constantly. Add rum (or not, as desired) and top with meringue as prepared above. To serve cold, pour directly from container, topping with meringue.

HOT MULLED CIDER

6 cups apple cider
½ cup light brown sugar
1 (2-inch) piece stick cinnamon
1 tsp. nutmeg
½ tsp. ginger
12 whole cloves
2 oranges, sliced
2 lemons, sliced

In a large saucepan, combine 6 cups apple cider, ½ cup light brown sugar, 1 (2-inch) piece stick cinnamon, 1 teaspoon nutmeg and ½ teaspoon ginger. Push 12 whole cloves into rinds of 2 oranges, sliced, and 2 lemons, sliced, using 2 cloves per slice. Bring mixture to a boil, stirring only to dissolve sugar. Reduce heat, cover and simmer 5 minutes. Makes 6 cups.

❊ *Note:* If apple cider is not available, apple juice (canned, bottled or frozen, reconstituted) may be substituted.

OLD ENGLISH SYLLABUB

3 eggs, separated
1 cup sugar
½ cup lemon juice
2 cups heavy cream, whipped

In blender container, whir 3 egg yolks until thick and lemon-colored. With motor still on, gradually add ¾ cup sugar and ½ cup lemon juice. In a medium bowl, beat 3 egg whites until frothy. Gradually add remaining ¼ cup sugar and beat until a thick, glossy meringue is formed. Fold egg yolk mixture into meringue. Add 2 cups heavy cream, whipped, and fold mixture together gently but thoroughly. Makes about 6 cups.

❊ *Note:* So rich and thick is this classic brew, it should be sipped through a large straw or eaten with a teaspoon.

HOT POSSET

4 eggs, separated
2 cups milk
2 cups light cream
¾ cup sugar
2 tsp. almond extract
1 tsp. grated lemon rind
1 cup Scotch whisky
½ cup chopped, toasted almonds

In large bowl of electric mixer, beat 4 egg yolks at high speed until thick and lemon-colored. In a large saucepan, heat 2 cups each milk and light cream and ½ cup sugar. Stirring to dissolve sugar, allow mixture to come to a simmer. Gradually pour mixture over egg yolks, beating constantly. Slowly beat in 2 teaspoons almond extract, 1 teaspoon grated lemon rind and 1 cup Scotch whisky.

In small bowl of electric mixer, beat egg whites (with clean beaters) until frothy. Add remaining ¼ cup sugar slowly, beating constantly, until a thick, glossy meringue is formed. Quickly fold meringue into hot mixture and serve at once with a sprinkle of ½ cup chopped, toasted almonds on each serving. Makes about 6 cups. *(See photograph.)*

SPICY CALIFORNIA PUNCH

4 cups unsweetened grapefruit juice
4 cups orange juice
2 cups honey
¼ cup lime juice
1 tsp. allspice
1 tsp. nutmeg

In a 3-qt. container, combine 4 cups each unsweetened grapefruit juice and orange juice, 2 cups honey, ¼ cup lime juice and 1 teaspoon each allspice and nutmeg. Let stand at room temperature 1 hour, to allow flavors to "marry". Chill. To serve, pour over ice in a punch bowl or in several pitchers. Makes 10 cups.

SPRITZER

2 cups (1 pt.) tawny port
1 cup club soda, chilled
6 thin orange slices
6 thin lemon slices
1 lime, cut into 6 wedges

In a 1-qt. pitcher, combine 2 cups tawny port and 1 cup club soda, chilled. Pour immediately over ice in 6 tall glasses into which 1 slice each of orange and lemon has been placed. Garnish each with a wedge of lime. Makes 3 cups.

GLÖGG

2 cups Burgundy wine
2 cups cranberry juice
1 cup dry sherry
1 cup vodka
16 sugar cubes

In a saucepan heat 2 cups each Burgundy wine and cranberry juice and 1 cup dry sherry. When very hot (but not boiling) stir in ½ cup vodka. Place a wire rack over saucepan and place a mound of sugar cubes (16) in center. Heat remaining ½ cup vodka in a small saucepan, ignite it and pour over sugar cubes on rack. Sugar cubes will burn and melt into drink. Serve hot. Makes 6 cups.

SHANDYGAFF

1 (12-oz.) can or bottle beer, well chilled
1 (7-oz.) bottle ginger ale, well chilled

Simultaneously pour half of 1 (12-oz.) can or bottle beer and half of 1 (7-oz.) bottle ginger ale into a chilled glass. In second chilled glass, repeat with remaining beer and ginger ale. Serve at once.

✳ *Note:* Ginger beer is traditionally used in this mildly alcoholic, refreshing quaff. If you can find it, do use it.

HOT MOCHA CREAM

6 (1-oz.) squares semi-sweet chocolate
1 cup boiling water
¼ cup sugar
5 cups milk
2 Tb. powdered instant coffee
1 Tb. cinnamon
2 tsp. vanilla extract
Marshmallows

Combine 6 (1-oz.) squares semi-sweet chocolate, 1 cup boiling water and ¼ cup sugar in top of double boiler. Place over hot (not boiling) water and cook, stirring constantly, until chocolate melts and mixture is well blended.

Meanwhile, in a large saucepan, combine 5 cups milk, 2 tablespoons powdered instant coffee, 1 tablespoon cinnamon and 2 teaspoons vanilla extract. Heat, stirring, until mixture comes to a simmer. Gradually add chocolate, beating with wire whisk or rotary beater, until well mixed. Serve hot, topped with a marshmallow. Makes 6 cups.

✳ Note: Instead of using semi-sweet chocolate squares, 1 (6-oz.) pkg. chocolate morsels may be substituted.

TEA PUNCH

6 cups, freshly brewed, orange-spice flavored tea (double strength)
1 cup honey
½ cup orange juice
¼ cup lemon juice

To 6 cups freshly brewed, orange-spice flavored tea (double strength) add 1 cup honey, ½ cup orange juice and ¼ cup lemon juice. Stir to dissolve honey. Chill. Makes 7¾ cups.

✳ Note: To serve hot, heat in upper part of double boiler (won't boil and become bitter that way).

COLA COW

3 (6-oz.) bottles cola beverage, chilled
3 cups milk
1 pt. vanilla ice cream

Pour 3 (6-oz.) bottles cola beverage, chilled, into a 1-qt. pitcher. Add 3 cups milk and stir once or twice. Pour into 6 tall glasses and add a scoop of vanilla ice cream to each glass.

❋ Note: It's important that the cola beverage be chilled for this recipe, to prevent it from becoming too fizzy and (shudder) to prevent the possibility of slight curdling. Also, you might try this recipe with coffee ice cream, instead of vanilla . . . equally fine.

CHAMPAGNE PUNCH

1 cup orange juice
1 cup maple blended syrup
½ cup lemon juice
½ cup brandy
½ cup maraschino cherry syrup
1 bottle champagne (⅘ qt.)
1 orange, thinly sliced
1 lemon, thinly sliced
1 lime, thinly sliced

In a large bowl or pitcher, combine 1 cup each orange juice and maple blended syrup, ½ cup each lemon juice, brandy and maraschino cherry syrup. Stir well to mix, then let stand at room temperature 1 hour to allow flavors to mingle. Chill. Just before serving, add 1 bottle champagne (⅘ qt.) and pour over ice in punch bowl. Garnish with thin slices of an orange, a lemon and a lime. Makes 8 cups. (See photograph.)

❋ Note: This is delightful without the champagne, too. The yield is 3½ cups.

IRISH COFFEE

2 tsp. sugar
Hot, strong, black coffee
2 Tb. Irish whiskey (1 jigger)
1 ½ Tb. whipped cream

For one serving: Rinse a stemmed Irish coffee goblet in hot water. Dry well. Put 2 teaspoons sugar in glass. Add 2 tablespoons hot, strong, black coffee and stir to dissolve sugar. Add 2 tablespoons Irish whiskey and enough of the remaining hot coffee to fill glass to within 1 inch from top. Gently spoon 1 ½ tablespoons whipped cream onto coffee and serve at once.

For 6 servings: Use 2 tablespoons sugar, ¾ cup Irish whiskey and ¼ cup heavy cream, whipped.

CAFÉ BRULOT

When a recipe calls for setting liquor gloriously ablaze, as this one does, be sure that you stand back when you ignite the spirits, as the flame may flare up briefly. And be sure nothing flammable is nearby as you light your potion.

1 cup brandy
¼ cup sugar
6 (2-inch) strips orange peel
3 (2-inch) strips lemon peel
2 (1-inch) pieces stick cinnamon
10 whole cloves
4 cups hot, strong, black coffee

In a medium saucepan, combine 1 cup brandy, ¼ cup sugar, 6 (2-inch) strips orange peel, 3 (2-inch) strips lemon peel, 2 (1-inch) pieces stick cinnamon and 10 whole cloves. Heat gently until warmed, then set aflame with match. Allow flame to burn for 1 minute, then slowly stir in 4 cups hot, strong, black coffee. Serve at once. Makes 5 cups. *(See photograph.)*

CRANBERRY NOG

2 cups (1 pt.) cranberry juice, well chilled
2 cups light cream, well chilled
1 cup honey

Combine 2 cups each cranberry juice and light cream, both well chilled, with 1 cup honey, beating well. Chill and serve over ice. Makes 5 cups. (See photograph.)

SCANDINAVIAN SWIZZLE

In this refreshing drink only the juice from a can of Bing cherries is used. You can sprinkle the cherries over vanilla ice cream for a lovely dessert.

1 (18-oz.) can unsweetened pineapple juice (2 ¼ cups)
1 ½ cups juice from 1 (30-oz.) can Bing cherries
1 cup orange juice
1 cup maple blended syrup
1 cup Cherry Heering liqueur
½ cup brandy
¼ cup lemon juice
1 qt. club soda, chilled

Combine 1 (18-oz.) can unsweetened pineapple juice, 1 ½ cups Bing cherry juice, 1 cup each orange juice, maple blended syrup and Cherry Heering liqueur, ½ cup brandy and ¼ cup lemon juice. Chill thoroughly. Just before serving stir in 1 qt. club soda, chilled. Serve over ice. Makes 2 ½ qts.

❉ Note: This is also marvellous served hot. To do so, omit club soda, and combine all other ingredients, heating them to a boil. Immediately remove from heat and serve. The yield will be reduced to 7 ½ cups.

SNOWBALL

2 ¼ cups commercial eggnog, chilled
¾ cup heavy cream, chilled
½ cup light rum
2 Tb. lemon juice
2 (7-oz.) bottles lime-lemon soda

In blender container, combine 2¼ cups commercial eggnog, chilled, ¾ cup heavy cream, chilled, ½ cup light rum and 2 tablespoons lemon juice. Whir 15 seconds, then divide mixture between 6 (6-oz.) saucer-shaped champagne glasses. Into each, pour about ¼ cup of the lime-lemon soda to foam the drink into a "snowball." Serve with short straws.

BOURBON HOT TODDY

1 ½ cups hot water
½ cup sugar
¼ cup lemon juice
¼ tsp. powdered cloves
1 ½ cups bourbon

In a saucepan, combine 1½ cups hot water, ½ cup sugar, ¼ cup lemon juice and ¼ teaspoon powdered cloves. Bring to a boil, stirring only to dissolve sugar. Remove from heat and stir in 1½ cups bourbon. Serve immediately. Makes about 3 cups.

❋ Note: Toddies may be served cold. Dissolve ½ cup sugar in ½ cup hot water. Add 1 cup cold water, lemon juice and cloves. Proceed as directed but do not boil. Add ice cubes and a garnish of mint if desired.

CHAPTER TEN / MENUS

The most important quality of every meal is its balance: light with heavy, sweet with tart, something crunchy, something creamy. Which vegetable to serve with what is not always the easy proposition it appears, so if you're in a muddle, our twelve traditional holiday menus will help. Each represents a basic style of holiday entertaining, and all the styles are here. Each menu, of course, may be varied according to taste, and served in whatever fashion best suits you, but the balance in each should be maintained. With a few small exceptions, all the recipes in each menu are in this book. A brief word about wines: the old rule says that red wine goes with beef, lamb, duck, goose and rich stews. White wine, being lighter, goes with more delicate fowl and fish. We do believe, however, that you should serve what you like best, and there's an easy-going trend afoot that agrees.

FESTIVE FALL DINNER

Seviche of Scallops (page 9)
Jellied Madrilène (page 22)
Stuffed Veal Shoulder (page 50)
Ratatouille (page 81)   Stir-Fried Asparagus (page 69)
Caesar Salad (page 90)
Maple Mousse (page 152)   Assorted Cookies (page 112)

THANKSGIVING

Bourbon Pâté (page 15)   Coconut Cheese Bites (page 4)
Angels in Blankets (page 2)
Double Mushroom Consommé (page 26)
Maple-Glazed Turkey with Pecan Cornbread Stuffing (page 38)
Potato Soufflé (page 77)   Buttery Baked Carrots (page 75)
Broccoli with Toasted, Salted Pecans (page 73)
Hearts of Palm and Radish Salad (page 88)
Pumpkin Pie (page 132)   Icy Lemons or Oranges (page 160)

LADIES' LUNCHEON

Belgian Endive with Zingara Sauce (page 82)
Hungarian Cherry Soup (page 27)
Veal Piccata with Saffron Rice (page 56)
Spinach and Bacon Salad (page 92)
Baked Alaska (page 146)

TRIM-THE-TREE PARTY

Mugs of Belgian Beer Soup (page 26)   Toasted Saltines
Devilled Beef Bones (page 61)
Roast Capon with Apple and Raisin Stuffing (page 40)
Onions Danish-Style (page 84)
Macaroni Salad (page 94)
Panettone (page 125)
Scandinavian Swizzle (page 176)

CHANUKAH DINNER

Chicken Liver Boats (page 14)
Standing Rib Roast (page 45)
Roast Capon with Apple and Raisin Stuffing (page 40)
Potato Pancakes   Broccoli   Carrots
Lebkuchen (page 117)   Mexican Fruit Bars (page 119)

GREEK CHRISTMAS CELEBRATION

Greek Salad (page 89)
Watercress Soup (page 27)
Roast Rack of Lamb (page 44)
Lemon Rice   Asparagus Spears   Broiled Tomatoes
Baklava (page 154)   Greek New Year's Bread (page 143)

CHRISTMAS EVE SUPPER

Caviar Croustade (page 8)
Burgundy Beef Soup (page 20)
Duck Montmorency (page 41)
Avocado Rice (page 71)
Hearts of Lettuce and Tomato (page 103)
Mincemeat Pear Pie (page 163)

CHRISTMAS DAY DINNER

Smoked Salmon and Avocado (page 7)
Watercress Soup (page 27)
Standing Rib Roast with Yorkshire Pudding (page 45)
Brussels Sprouts with Chestnut Sauce (page 74)
Celery Amandine (page 84)
Oven Roast Potatoes (page 45)
Pear Salad with O'Henry's Dressing (page 97)
Christmas Pudding (page 126) with Hard Sauce

NEW YEAR'S EVE BUFFET

Escargots (page 2)   Van Dyke Radishes with Green Butter (page 3)
Caviar Eggs (page 4)
Ham with Brandied Cream Cheese Glaze (page 49)
Steak and Kidney Pie with Oysters (page 48)
German Potato Salad (page 91)   Waldorf Salad (page 97)
Cranberries in Snow (page 162)   Maple Chiffon Pie (page 165)
Ginger Claret Punch (page 168)   Spicy California Punch (page 171)
Bourbon Hot Toddy (page 177)

NEW YEAR'S DAY BRUNCH

Old English Syllabub (page 170)   Champagne Punch (page 174)
Blanquette of Poultry (page 42)
Almond Wild Rice (page 57)
Fruit Melba (page 163)
Italian Almond Kisses (page 112)   Irish Mince Pies (page 116)
Edelweiss Cookies (page 118)

HOLIDAY OPEN HOUSE

Crabmeat Quiche (page 5)   Baby Burgers on Mini-Biscuits (page 6)
Guacamole with Winter Vegetables (page 7)
Cassoulet (page 58)
Vermont Beef Brisket (page 63)
Göteburg Limpa (page 131)
Christmas Slaw (page 101)   Artichoke, Shrimp and Rice Salad (page 94)
Macédoine of Winter Fruits (page 164)   Coeur à la Crème (page 152)
Gingerbread Stollen (page 124)   Colonial Virginia Cake (page 138)
Hot Mulled Cider (page 170)   Cranberry Nog (page 176)

TWELFTH NIGHT DINNER

Ham Rouladen in Piquant Maple Sauce (page 10)
Bayou Bisque (page 29)
Beef Wellington (page 65)
Baked Acorn Squash (page 72)   Sesame Spinach (page 85)
Avocado and Grapefruit Salad (page 88)
Triple Chocolate Torte (page 129)
Café Brulot (page 175)

TABLE OF WEIGHTS AND MEASURES

For your information . . .

1 teaspoon	= ⅓ tablespoon
1 tablespoon	= 3 teaspoons
2 tablespoons	= 1 ounce (1 jigger)
4 tablespoons	= ¼ cup
5⅓ tablespoons	= ⅓ cup
8 tablespoons	= ½ cup
16 tablespoons	= 1 cup
1 cup	= ½ pint
2 cups	= 1 pint (1 pound)
2 pints	= 1 quart (2 pounds)
4 quarts	= 1 gallon (8 pounds)
16 ounces	= 1 pound
16 fluid ounces	= 1 pint (2 cups)

At one time or another, it's happened to us all: a recipe is carefully, lovingly prepared, and yet it fails. Often the problem is improper measuring of ingredients, particularly in baking. With this in mind, watch for:

1. Dry ingredients, such as flour and sugar, should always be measured in aluminum measuring cups which are marked accurately as to capacity. Never measure dry ingredients in glass, which is for liquid, or in china teacups.

2. Always measure liquid ingredients at eye level (not overhead, or on the table) in a glass measuring cup. For small amounts, you might prefer to use a tablespoon. Worth memorizing: an 8-oz. measuring cup equals 16 tablespoons; 1 ounce is 2 tablespoons; ¼ cup is 4 tablespoons.

3. Never sift flour directly into the measuring cup. Pockets of air may form, which could wreak havoc with your efforts. Instead, sift flour onto a piece of waxed paper or aluminum foil, then measure out what you need.

4. Never pack flour into measuring cup or measuring spoon. Spoon or scoop it lightly into the cup and level the top with the edge of a spatula or straight-edged knife. DO pack brown sugar (with the back of a spoon).

5. Always measure out flat spoonfuls of dry ingredients—never heaping. Level, if necessary, with the edge of a spatula. By the way, table cutlery is not for measuring: you should have two sets of standard measuring spoons. (Don't measure flavorings and such directly over bowl . . . spillage, you know.) By the way, it might help to know that 3 teaspoons equal 1 tablespoon.

INDEX OF RECIPES BY CHAPTER

APPETIZERS AND CANAPES
Angels in Blankets, 2, 32-33
Baby Burgers on Mini-Biscuits, 6
Bacon-Mushroom Bouchées, 9
Beef Lindstrom, 17
Blue Cheese Canapes, 8
Bourbon Pâté, 15
Cauliflowerettes,
    Sautéed, 3, 32-33
Caviar Croustade, 8, 32-33
Caviar Eggs, 4, 32-33
Chicken Liver Boats, 14
Coconut Cheese Bites, 4
Crabmeat Quiche, 5
Escargots, 2, 32-33
Garlic-Salted Nibbles, 4
Guacamole with Winter
    Vegetables, 7
Ham Rouladen in Piquant
    Maple Sauce, 10
Hors d'Oeuvre Provençal, 13
Olives and Mushrooms
    Aegean, 13, 32-33
Pork, Hawaiian Curried, 11
Radishes, Van Dyke, with
    Green Butter, 3, 32-33
Salmon Pâté, 15
Salmon, Smoked, and Avocado, 7
Scallops, Seviche of, 9, 32-33
Turkey Salad with Sautéed
    Walnuts, 12
Vegetable Hors d'Oeuvre with
    Chicken Liver Stuffing, 16

SOUPS
Bayou Bisque, 29
Beef and Ale Soup, 35
Belgian Beer Soup, 26
Black Bean Soup with Rum
    and Maple, 23
Bookbinder's Shrimp
    Chowder, 22, 31
Borscht, Quick, with Potato, 23
Burgundy Beef Soup, 20, 34
Cherry Soup, Hungarian, 27
Chinese Soup, 25
Cholodnik, White Russian, 28
Cock-A-Leekie Soup, 21
Corn Soup, Navajo, 28
Eggnog Soup, 20
Madrilène, Jellied, 22
Mushroom Consommé, Double, 26
Purée Mongole, 30
Rindsuppe (Brown Beef Soup), 35
Sausage and Onion Soup, 24
Shrimp and Oyster Chowder, 30
Watercress Soup, 27

MEATS
Beef Bones, Devilled, 61
Beef Brisket, Vermont, 63
Beef Wellington, 64
Blanquette of Poultry, 44
Capon, Roast, with Apple and
    Raisin Stuffing, 40
Cassoulet, 58
Duck Montmorency, 41

Flank Steak, Mexican, 60
Goose, Roast, with Sage and
    Onion Stuffing, 42
Ham en Croûte with Madeira
    Sauce, 46
Ham with Brandied Cream
    Cheese Glaze, 49
Ham with Gelatine Glaze, 47
Lamb, Roast Rack of, 43, 52-53
Lobster Tails, see Steak Neptune
Pork Chops, Stuffed, with
    Maple-Orange Sauce, 59
Rib Roast, Standing, with
    Yorkshire Pudding, 45
Roasting Chart, 65
Steak and Kidney Pie with
    Oysters, 48, 52-53
Steak Neptune, 62
Turkey, Maple-Glazed, with
    Pecan Cornbread Stuffing, 38
Veal Piccata with Saffron Rice, 56
Veal Shoulder, Stuffed, 50
Vitello Tonnato, 55
Wild Almond Rice, 57

VEGETABLES
Acorn Squash, Baked, 72
Almond Wild Rice, 57
Asparagus, Stir-Fried, 69
Avocado and Corn, 70
Bean Sprouts Orientale, 71
Beets, Sweet and Sour, 68
Broccoli with Toasted, Salted
    Pecans, 73
Brussels Sprouts with Chestnut
    Sauce, 74
Cabbage and Cream, 75
Carrots, Buttery Baked, 75
Carrots, Oven Crisped, 85
Celery Amandine, 84
Colcannon, 76
Corn Puffle, 80
Endive, Belgian, with Zingara
    Sauce, 54, 82

Green Beans Supreme, 70
Kohlrabi Smitane, 83
Onions Danish-Style, 84
Potato Soufflé, 77
Pumpkin Fritters, 79
Ratatouille, 51, 81
Red Cabbage Normand, 78
Rice, Avocado, 71
Rice, Saffron, 57
Spinach, Sesame, 85
Spinach-Stuffed Squash, 72
Zucchini, Batter-Fried, 78

SALADS
Artichoke, Shrimp and
    Rice Salad, 94
Avocado and Grapefruit
    Salad, 88
Beef Vinaigrette, 93
Caesar Salad, 90
Crab Louis, 98
Endive and Pineapple Salad, 100
Greek Salad, 89
Hearts of Lettuce and Tomato, 103
Hearts of Palm and
    Radish Salad, 88
Herring and Potato Salad, 101
Macaroni Salad, 94
Mexican Salad, 96, 102
Okra and Oyster Salad, 89
Orange and Onion
    Salad, 95, 103
Pear Salad with O'Henry's
    Dressing, 97
Potato Salad, German, 91
Salad Johannes, 100
Slaw, Christmas, 101
Spinach and Bacon Salad, 92
Three-Bean Salad with
    Cervelat, 99
Waldorf Salad, 97

CONFECTIONS
Almond Calissons, 107

Apricot-Coconut Squares, 111
Fudge, Snowy Day, 106
Ginger-Stuffed Dates, 107 ·
Kumquats, Stuffed, 111
Marzipan, Mock, 108
Molasses Taffy,
   Old-Fashioned, 109
Peanut Butter Crisps, 110
Penuche, 110
Sesame Seed Brittle, 108
Turkish Delight, 106

COOKIES
Almond Kisses, Italian, 112
Chocolate-Maple Bourbon
   Balls, 121
Dutch Yule Cookies, 116
Eccles Cakes, 120
Edelweiss Cookies, *113*, 118
Fruit Bars, Mexican, 119
Lebkuchen, 117
Macaroons, Christmas, 112
Mince Pies, Irish ,*113*, 116
Snowball Cookies, 121
Spritz Wreaths, *113*, 116
Tyrolean Springerli, 115

BREAD AND CAKES
Apple-Marzipan Kuchen, 130
Bagels, 134
Bûche de Noël, 142
Challah, 135
Coffee Cake, Holiday, 141
Colonial Virginia Cake, 138
Fruit Cake, Traditional, 126
Gingerbread Stollen, 124
Greek New Year's Bread, 143
Honey Cake (Lekach), 137
Hungarian Poppy Seed Cake, 128
Kranzer, Frankfurter, 133
Limpa, Göteburg, 131
Martha Washington's Great
   Cake, 139
Norwegian Christmas Breads, 127

Panettone, 125
Prince Phillip Cake, 140
Pumpkin Pie, 132
Three Kings' Loaf, 136
Triple Chocolate Torte, 129

DESSERTS
Baba au Rhum with Maple, 148
Baked Alaska, 146
Baklava, 154
Chestnut Soufflé, 153
Coeur à la Crème, 152
Cranberries in Snow, *114*, 162
Crème Amandine, 164
Flaming Angel Cake, 160
Fruit Melba, 163
Ice Cream Puffs with
   Chocolate Glaze, 151
Icy Lemons, *156-157*, 160
Lemon-Raspberry Parfait, 159
Macédoine of Winter Fruits, 164
Maple Chiffon Pie, 165
Maple Mousse, 152
Mincemeat Pear Pie, 163
Oeufs à la Neige, 149
Orange Bavarian, *114*, 165
Paris Brest, 150
Queen of Puddings, *114*, 161
Riz Royale, Maple, 147, *156-157*

DRINKS
Bourbon Hot Toddy, 177
Café Brulot, *155*, 175
California Punch, Spicy, 171
Champagne Punch, *158*, 174
Cola Cow, 174
Cranberry Nog, *158*, 176
Eggnog, Hot (or Cold), 169
Ginger Claret Punch, 168
Glögg, 172
Irish Coffee, 175
Mocha Cream, Hot, 173
Mulled Cider, Hot, 170

Posset, Hot, *158,* 171
Santa's Nightcap, 168
Scandinavian Swizzle, 176
Shandygaff, 172
Snowball, 177
Spritzer, 172
Syllabub, Old English, 170
Tea Punch, 173

SAUCES AND GLAZES,
STUFFINGS AND DRESSINGS
Apple and Raisin Stuffing, 40
Brandied Cream Cheese
    Glaze, 49
Buttercream Frosting, 117

Chestnut Sauce, 74
Chicken Liver Stuffing, 16
Chocolate Glaze, 151
Devil's Sauce, 61
Madeira Sauce, 46
Maple-Orange Sauce, 59
Maple Sauce, 10
O'Henry's Salad Dressing, 97
Pecan Cornbread Stuffing, 38
Sage and Onion Stuffing, 43
Spinach Stuffing, 72
Streusel, 141
Tuna Sauce, 55
Yorkshire Pudding, 45
Zingara Sauce, *54,* 82

Acorn Squash, Baked, 72
Ale Soup, Beef and, 35
Almond Calissons, 107
Almond Kisses, Italian, 112
Almond Wild Rice, 57
Angel Cake, Flaming, 160
Angels in Blankets
(Shrimp), 2, 32-33
APPETIZERS AND
CANAPES, 1-17
Apple and Raisin Stuffing, 40
Apple-Marzipan Kuchen, 130
Apricot-Coconut Squares, 111
Artichoke, Shrimp and
Rice Salad, 94
Asparagus, Stir-Fried, 69
Avocado and Corn, 70
Avocado and Grapefruit
Salad, 88
Avocado Rice, 71
Avocado, Smoked Salmon and, 7

Baba au Rhum with Maple, 148
Bacon Salad, Spinach and, 92
Bacon-Mushroom Bouchées, 9
Bagels, 134
Baked Alaska, 146
Baklava, 154
Bayou Bisque, 29
Beans, Green, Supreme, 70
Bean Sprouts Orientale, 71
Beef and Ale Soup, 35
Beef Bones, Devilled, 61
Beef Brisket, Vermont, 63
Beef, Brown, Soup
(Rindsuppe), 35
Beef Lindstrom, 17
Beef, Rib Roast of, with
Yorkshire Pudding, 45
Beef Soup, Burgundy, 20, 34
Beef Vinaigrette, 93
Beef Wellington, 64

Beer Soup, Belgian, 26
Beets, Sweet and Sour, 68
Black Bean Soup with Rum
and Maple, 23
Blanquette of Poultry, 44
Blue Cheese Canapes, 8
Bookbinder's Shrimp
Chowder, 22, 31
Borscht, Quick, with Potato, 23
Bourbon Balls,
Chocolate-Maple, 121
Bourbon Pâté, 15
Bourbon Hot Toddy, 177
Brandied Cream Cheese
Glaze, 49
BREADS AND CAKES, 123-143
Broccoli with Toasted, Salted
Pecans, 73
Brussels Sprouts with Chestnut
Sauce, 74
Bûche de Noël, 142
Burgundy Beef Soup, 20, 34
Burgers, Baby, on Mini-Biscuits, 6
Buttercream Frosting, 117

Cabbage and Cream, 75
Caesar Salad, 90
Café Brulot, 155, 175
CAKES, 123-143
Cake, Colonial Virginia, 138
Cakes, Eccles, 120
Cake, Hungarian Poppy
Seed, 128
Cake, Martha Washington's
Great, 139
Cake, Prince Phillip, 140
CANAPES, 1-17
CANDY, 106-111
Capon, Roast, with Apple and
Raisin Stuffing, 40
Carrots, Buttery Baked, 75
Carrots, Oven Crisped, 85

Cassoulet, 58
Cauliflowerettes,
  Sautéed, 3, 32-33
Caviar Croustade, 8, 32-33
Caviar Eggs, 4, 32-33
Celery Amandine, 84
Cervelat, Three-Bean Salad
  with, 99
Challah, 135
Champagne Punch, 158, 174
Cherry Soup, Hungarian, 27
Chestnut Sauce, 74
Chestnut Soufflé, 153
Chicken Liver Boats, 14
Chicken Liver Stuffing, 16
Chinese Soup, 25
Chocolate Glaze, 151
Chocolate-Maple Bourbon
  Balls, 121
Chocolate Torte, Triple, 129
Cholodnik, White Russian, 28
Christmas Breads,
  Norwegian, 127
Christmas Macaroons, 112
Christmas Pudding, 126
Christmas Slaw, 101
Cider, Hot Mulled, 170
Claret, Ginger, Punch, 168
Cock-A-Leekie Soup, 21
Coconut Cheese Bites, 4; see also
  Apricot-Coconut Squares
Coeur à la Crème, 152
Coffee Cake, Holiday, 141
Cola Cow, 174
Colcannon, 76
CONFECTIONS &
  COOKIES, 105-121
Corn, Avocado and, 70
Corn Puffle, 80
Corn Soup, Navajo, 28
Crab Louis, 98
Crabmeat Quiche, 5
Cranberries in Snow, 114, 162
Cranberry Nog, 158, 176

Cream Cheese Glaze,
  Brandied, 49
Cream Puff Pastry, 151
Crème Amandine, 164

Dates, Ginger-Stuffed, 107
DESSERTS, 145-165
Devilled Beef Bones, 61
Devil's Sauce, 61
DRINKS, 167-177
Duck Montmorency, 41
Dutch Yule Cookies, 116

Eccles Cakes, 120
Edelweiss Cookies, 113, 118
Eggnog, Hot (or Cold), 169
Eggnog Soup, 20
Eggs, Caviar, 4, 32-33
Endive and Pineapple Salad, 100
Endive, Belgian, with Zingara
  Sauce, 54, 82
Escargots, 2, 32-33

Flaming Angel Cake, 160
Flank Steak, Mexican, 60
Frosting, Buttercream, 117
Fruit Bars, Mexican, 119
Fruit Cake, Traditional, 126
Fruit Melba, 163
Fudge, Snowy Day, 106

Garlic-Salted Nibbles, 4
Gingerbread Stollen, 124
Ginger Claret Punch, 168
Ginger-Stuffed Dates, 107
Glögg, 172
Goose, Roast, with Sage and
  Onion Stuffing, 42
Grapefruit and Avocado
  Salad, 88
Greek New Year's Bread, 143
Greek Salad, 89
Green Beans Supreme, 70
Guacamole with Winter
  Vegetables, 7

194

Ham en Croûte, 46
Ham Rouladen in Piquant
   Maple Sauce, 10
Ham with Brandied Cream
   Cheese Glaze, 49
Ham with Gelatine Glaze, 47
Hearts of Lettuce and
   Tomato, 103
Hearts of Palm and Radish
   Salad, 88
Herring and Potato Salad, 101
Honey Cake (Lekach), 137
Hors d'Oeuvre Provençal, 13

Ice Cream Puffs with
   Chocolate Glaze, 151
Irish Coffee, 175
Irish Mince Pies, 113, 116

Kidney Pie, Steak and, with
   Oysters, 48, 52-53
Kohlrabi Smitane, 83
Kranzer, Frankfurter, 133
Kumquats, Stuffed, 111

Lamb, Roast Rack of, 43, 52-53
Lebkuchen, 117
Lekach (Honey Cake), 137
Lemons, Icy, 156-157, 160
Lemon-Raspberry Parfait, 159
Lettuce, Hearts of, and
   Tomato, 103
Limpa, Göteburg, 131
Loaf, Three Kings', 136
Lobster Tails (Steak Neptune), 62

Macaroni Salad, 94
Macaroons, Christmas, 112
Macédoine of Winter Fruits, 164
Madeira Sauce, 46
Madrilène, Jellied, 22
Maple Chiffon Pie, 165
Maple Mousse, 152
Maple-Orange Sauce, 59

Maple Sauce, 10
Marzipan, Mock, 108; see also
   Apple-Marzipan Kuchen
Measuring, 186-187
MEATS, 37-65; Roasting Chart, 65
MENUS, 179-185
Mexican Salad, 96, 102
Mincemeat Pear Pie, 163
Mince Pies, Irish, 113, 116
Mocha Cream, Hot, 173
Molasses Taffy,
   Old-Fashioned, 109
Mushrooms and Olives
   Aegean, 13, 32-33; see also
   Bacon-Mushroom Bouchées
Mushroom Consommé, Double, 26

Oeufs à la Neige, 149
O'Henry's Salad Dressing, 97
Okra and Oyster Salad, 89
Olives and Mushrooms
   Aegean, 13, 32-33
Onion and Sage Stuffing, 43
Onions Danish-Style, 84
Onion Soup, Sausage and, 24
Orange and Onion
   Salad, 95, 103
Orange Bavarian, 114, 165
Oyster and Okra Salad, 89
Oyster Chowder, Shrimp and, 30
Oysters, Steak and Kidney
   Pie with, 48, 52-53

Palm, Hearts of, and
   Radish Salad, 88
Panettone, 125
Parfait, Lemon-Raspberry, 159
Paris Brest, 150
Pâté, Bourbon, 15
Pâté, Salmon, 15
Peaches (Salad Johannes), 100
Peanut Butter Crisps, 110
Pear Salad with O'Henry's
   Dressing, 97

195

Pecan Cornbread
  Stuffing, 38, *52-53*
Pecans, Broccoli with, 73
Penuche, 110
Pineapple and Endive Salad, 100
Poppy Seed Cake,
  Hungarian, 128
Pork Chops, Stuffed, with
  Maple-Orange Sauce, 59
Pork, Hawaiian Curried, 11
Posset, Hot, *158,* 171
Potato Salad, German, 91
Potato Salad, Herring and, 101
Potato Soufflé, 77
Poultry, Blanquette of, 44
Poultry Stuffings, see
  Stuffings Index, 191
Puddings, Queen of, *114,* 161
Pumpkin Fritters, 79
Pumpkin Pie, 132
Punch, Champagne, *158,* 174
Punch, Ginger Claret, 168
Punch, Spicy California, 171
Punch, Tea, 173
Purée Mongole, 30

Radishes, Van Dyke, with
  Green Butter, 3, *32-33*
Radish Salad, Hearts of Palm
  and, 88
Raisin and Apple Stuffing, 40
Raspberry Lemon Parfait, 159
Ratatouille, *51,* 81
Red Cabbage Normand, 78
Rib Roast, Standing, with
  Yorkshire Pudding, 45
Rice, Almond Wild, 57
Rice, Avocado, 71
Rice Salad, Artichoke,
  Shrimp and, 94
Rice, Saffron, 57
Rindsuppe (Brown Beef Soup), 35
Riz Royale, Maple, 147, *156-157*

Saffron Rice, 57
Sage and Onion Stuffing, 43
Salad Johannes, 100
Salmon Pâté, 15
Salmon, Smoked, and Avocado, 7
SALADS, 87-103
Santa's Nightcap, 168
Sauce, Chestnut, 74
Sauce, Maple, 10
Sauce, Maple-Orange, 59
Sauce, Zingara, 82
Sausage and Onion Soup, 24
Scallops, Seviche of, 9, *32-33*
Scandinavian Swizzle, 176
Sesame Seed Brittle, 108
Sesame Spinach, 85
Shandygaff, 172
Shrimp and Oyster
  Chowder, 30
Shrimp (Angels in
  Blankets), 2, *32-33*
Shrimp and Rice Salad,
  Artichoke, 94
Shrimp Chowder,
  Bookbinder's, 22, *31*
Slaw, Christmas, 101
Snowball, 177
Snowball Cookies, 121
SOUPS, 19-35
Spinach and Bacon Salad, 92
Spinach, Sesame, 85
Spinach-Stuffed Squash, 72
Springerli, Tyrolean, 115
Spritzer, 172
Spritz Wreaths, *113,* 120
Squash, Acorn, Spinach-
  Stuffed, 72
Steak and Kidney Pie with
  Oysters, 48, *52-53*
Steak, Mexican Flank, 60
Steak Neptune, 62
Stollen, Gingerbread, 124

Streusel, 141
Stuffings, see Stuffings
  Index, 191
Syllabub, Old English, 170

Tea Punch, 173
Three-Bean Salad with
  Cervelat, 99
Toddy, Bourbon Hot, 177
Tomato, Hearts of Lettuce
  and, 103
Tuna Sauce, 55
Turkey, Maple-Glazed, with Pecan
  Cornbread Stuffing, 38, 52-53
Turkey Salad with Sautéed
  Walnuts, 12
Turkish Delight, 106
Tyrolean Springerli, 115

Veal Piccata with Saffron
  Rice, 56
Veal Shoulder, Stuffed, 50
VEGETABLES, 57, 67-85;
  see also SALADS
Vegetable Hors d'Oeuvre with
  Chicken Liver Stuffing, 16
Vitello Tonnato, 55

Waldorf Salad, 97
Watercress Soup, 27
Weights and Measures,
  Table of, 187
Wild Rice, Almond, 57

Yorkshire Pudding, 45

Zingara Sauce, 54, 82
Zucchini, Batter Fried, 78